Multiple Income Streams

How to Achieve Financial Independence in the 21ˢᵗ Century

Dan King

Mohit Tater

Copyright © 2017 by Dan King and Mohit Tater

This book is licensed for your personal enjoyment only. This book may not be re-sold or given away to other people. If you would like to share this book with another person, please purchase an additional copy for each recipient. If you're reading this book and did not purchase it, or it was not purchased for your use only, then please purchase your own copy. Thank you for respecting the hard work of this author.

All Rights Reserved. No part of this book may be reproduced in any form or by any electronic or mechanical means including information storage and retrieval systems without permission in writing from the publisher, except by a reviewer who may quote brief passages in a review.

For queries, please contact the authors by email at mohit@mohittater.com and dan@danmking.com.

Table of Contents

Introduction – What are multiple income streams and why should you build them? 1

What are multiple income streams? 2

Why you should build multiple income streams 3

Why should employees build multiple income streams? 5

By contrast, How about entrepreneurs? 7

How do we mitigate risk? 9

How this book is organized 11

Who we are 15

    Dan's Bio 15

    Mohit's Bio 24

Passive, Active and Hybrid Income Streams 31

The Multiple Income Streams Method (MIS Method) 37

Self-Awareness 41

    Self-Awareness Tool #1: Myers-Briggs 44

    Self-Awareness Tool #2: Meditation 53

    Self-Awareness Tool #3: Journaling 64

    Self-Awareness Tool #4: Long Walks 67

    Self-Awareness Tool #5: Asking Others 70

    Self-Awareness Tool #6: Cognitive Behavioral Therapy 73

Following-Up: A Self-Awareness Cheat Sheet 76

Self-Awareness Cheat Sheet 77

The Culmination of your Self-Awareness Efforts: The Unique Ability Concept 80

12 Creative Income Stream Ideas and how to Raise Money for Them 83

    Niche Websites 84

    Digital Products 88

    Prediction Markets 96

    University Tutoring 99

    Real Estate 103

    P2P Lending 112

    Intellectual Property and Royalties 119

    Freelancing 126

    Coaching 135

    Sharing Economy (AirBnB, Uber) 143

    Crowdfunding 153

    Raising Capital 157

Productivity **158**

    Virtual Assistant/Personal Assistant 159

    Blocking Distractions and Keeping Momentum 160

    Email Best Practices 162

    Goals 164

    Working Based on Your Body Cycle 166

    Stop Picking Up the Phone 168

Stay Healthy 169

Making Deadline and Cancelling Appointments 170

Impact vs. Effort 171

Identify Your Hurdles 172

Using Cloud Based Services 173

Running Multiple Businesses and Building a Team 174

Success starts with the right attitude 175

Come up with a plan 176

Monitor all your businesses closely 177

One business is good for a start 180

Consider future prospects 181

Pick your business partners wisely 182

Learn to work with freelancers 183

Create a To-Do list 184

Consult with other successful entrepreneurs 186

Exploit your own skills 187

Diversify in choosing your team 188

Keep your spirits high 189

Bring your team together 190

Allocate particular roles to each team member 191

Clearly outline the objectives of each task 193

Encourage employee feedback 194

Streamline communication channels 195

The greater picture 196

Know your employees 197

Listen and learn from your employees 198

Encourage innovation 199

Give a sense of ownership 200

Appreciate good performance 201

A chance for personal development 202

Conclusion 203

Thank You 204

Introduction – What are multiple income streams and why should you build them?

Let us tell you why we love to talk multiple income streams. It's because we think it represents the best possible risk/return approach to financial planning. Even if you spend the bulk of your career on one mission or one project, your financial plan can be significantly improved by building multiple income streams. But before we talk about why you need multiple income streams, let's be completely clear on what they are.

What are multiple income streams?

An income stream is everything from a filing clerk job to a multibillion-dollar technology start-up to a lemonade stand in a suburban neighbourhood. It's a catchall term for any mechanism for profit. One of the wisest possible financial allocations of some of our all-important scarce resources, time, is to learn about the many possible income streams in 2017 and how to create new ones. If you think of your career, in terms of multiple income streams, your whole perspective changes. You no longer define yourself by your business or your job but as someone seeking greater upside and less risk. You're now free to move about the monopoly board however you wish.

Why you should build multiple income streams

Dan currently has six income streams. Mohit has seven. The average millionaire has seven. We don't know how many income streams you should have. It depends on a whole host of factors specific to your life. We think most people can and should build multiple income streams regardless of your job situation, your financial situation, your marital status or how many kids you have. There are many reasons. But one reason alone takes the cake: risk mitigation. In a recent podcast, Ken Courtright said that:

"Here's a question: Did you know that having one main source of income leads to failure 100% of the time? I want to say this differently. Did you know that having one main source of income—that is 80% of your income or more—leads to failure, meaning death, 100% of the time?

100% of the time! So, at some point – maybe not tomorrow, but at some point – whatever you do will no longer add enough value to the world to sustain your lifestyle. The problem is that it's very difficult to predict when things will change. And even if that change does not occur during your lifetime, whatever sustains you probably has a limited upside.

When planning our careers, most of us decide to become employees or entrepreneurs. Those of us that prioritize stability prefer the safety of a standard, 9-5 job. Those of us that prefer the adrenaline and risk-rich entrepreneurial path start our own businesses. Most people in both camps rely exclusively on one or two income streams. Let's talk about why both employees and entrepreneurs should build multiple income streams.

Why should employees build multiple income streams?

Employees, in 2017, cannot expect baby boomer like stability throughout their careers. Technology is no longer its own industry; technology encompasses every industry. Some of the most old-school, traditional industries on earth have been disrupted at the flick of a switch. The hotel and taxi industries are two obvious examples. Recent research suggests that the idea that corporate America is downsizing like crazy is exaggerated so we're not saying you will be fired tomorrow.[1] But, when disruption happens, it happens far more quickly than it used to. And the internet offers tremendous opportunity for ambitious employees to build alternative income streams almost as quickly. If you've knowledge to share or money to invest in the right project, the financial world is your oyster.

If you've a blue-collar background, your job is at greater risk than ever. In the 2016 election, the media

---

[1] http://www.nationalaffairs.com/publications/detail/the-future-of-work

reported on coal miners in Pennsylvania who spent their entire lives doing blue-collar work only to lose their jobs. There's no doubt that economic globalization hastens the speed and extent of outsourcing as more and more physical labor can be done at lower cost in the developing world while those who prefer an ostensibly safer career as an employee may not find safety in 9-to-5 jobs. And most employees have limited financial upside even if they manage to stay in their jobs for the remainder of their careers, <u>provided that they do not build multiple income streams.</u>

By contrast, How about entrepreneurs?

Entrepreneurs are glorified by our popular culture. Suddenly, they are no longer the boring, stuffy, business people of old, carrying their overflowing briefcases from one Radisson to the next. Entrepreneurs are now smart, sexy, t-shirt wearing, Silicon Valley superhero adventurers, easily solving the world's biggest problems and retiring at 27.

This stereotype accurately describes only a small percentage of entrepreneurs. Many entrepreneurs do not build technology businesses – they run convenience stores on our street corners and restaurants in suburban strip malls. Entrepreneurship is not synonymous with technology start-ups that scale from 0 to a billion dollars in the blink of an eye. We think so because our university classes on entrepreneurship are about technology start-ups as technology start-ups can scale more quickly than traditional businesses. But even those entrepreneurs, dead-set on building the next unicorn, rarely achieve their goals. If they do, there is little doubt that wealth and success, on an inconceivable scale, can be theirs... But the odds are not great.

Everyone wants to get rich from the trend of fast-scaling technology start-ups. In the rush to invest in these companies, many people miss an important point: That start-up investing is even riskier than you can imagine. Any company that can scale up faster than the speed of light can crash just as quickly. And when a company crashes, you know what happens to your hard-earned money. Mohit can attest to this first hand because as an angel investor, he has both lost and made money investing in start-ups. So, if we cut through all the mythology and all the bullshit, we are left with an extremely risky proposition.

How do we mitigate risk?

How do we mitigate risk if we are confronted with it whether we are employees or entrepreneurs? We do what every financial advisor worth his or her salt tells us to do: we diversify. If you've an investment advisor, he or she has probably told you that you should not put all your eggs in one basket. That makes sense because you can't imagine investing all your savings in one stock. You intuitively understand why this is a bad idea; just like the start-up in the last paragraph, the public company could come crashing down. It could happen because of a corruption scandal or perhaps good old-fashioned fraud.[2] The public company rarely crashes as quickly as a technology start-up but it is still vulnerable to the whims of fate.

So, we suspect you agree with us that you shouldn't invest all your savings in one stock. But there's a much greater chance that you're not applying the principle of diversification to your finances, more generally. If

---

[2] https://en.wikipedia.org/wiki/Bre-X#Fraud_exposed

diversification truly limits risk in the stock market, why wouldn't it lower our financial risk, more generally? Why not earn income from multiple sources?

Now that you understand the what and why of multiple income streams, let us tell you how this book is organized so you can get the most out of it.

How this book is organized

We start with mini-biographies of the authors to answer the question of why you should listen to what we have to say about multiple income streams. Next, we discuss how you can get off to a good start by determining how much you are willing to invest of the two most valuable resources, time and money. The answer to that question will dictate your ideal combination of active and passive income streams. Rather than setting out wantonly to make as much money as possible, we want to be deliberate in building a plan that works for you.

Then we'll discuss the three-step method, which we call the multiple income streams method or the MIS method – the three big picture steps we took to get where we are. They are:

1. Developing a clear understanding of our business strengths and weaknesses .
2. Exposing ourselves to deeply creative income stream ideas.

3. Creating very powerful, personally-tailored productivity systems to implement what we've learned.

We'll then jump into a discussion about self-awareness, the hidden weapon in any successful entrepreneur's arsenal. We acknowledge that people's skill sets are radically different from one another. Some people are more cut out to be business people than others but the central logic of business is so simple that everyone has significant strengths to bring to the table. Not everyone is *ready* to use their gifts productively but being clear on what they, and your imperfections are, is an extremely powerful first step.

Once you know what you're really good at, it's about matching your strengths and weaknesses with one of the many creative income stream ideas that are easier to implement than ever before. We're going to discuss ten specific income stream ideas, many of which you've likely not heard of, along with ways to raise capital for some of the more passive income stream ideas – as passive income streams require more money than labor. You'll want to build a portfolio of one or more of these income streams or head to the Internet or networking groups to learn about additional ideas if you dislike all these. Dan's site, www.multipleincomestreamshub.com, is a great source for additional ideas.

With an honest knowledge of your true abilities and some great income stream ideas in your pocket, it's now time to implement what you've learned. This is easier said than done. How many times have you gotten excited but a new idea or lifestyle change only to see your enthusiasm suddenly diminish at the first sign of trouble, or simply the need to roll up your sleeves and do some old-fashioned, hard work? There's no need to be ashamed – that's human nature – particularly so in the distraction age when there are so many forces that diminish your productivity.

The answer is to combine your newfound self-knowledge with productivity systems that range from the cutting edge to the super simple. Like anything in business, it's about testing, testing, testing. We will give you a bunch of systems that work for us. You may like them or you may prefer other systems. It doesn't matter so long as you continue searching for productivity systems that empower you to get more and more done. Otherwise, you'll be wasting your time. <u>The last thing we want is for you to fail to act</u> as that's why most people fail to create the lives of their dreams. We encourage you to dream but you must, one day, wake from those dreams and work hard to make them a reality.

Who we are

We are two millennial entrepreneurs who have built unconventional, creative six-figure careers with multiple income streams. This book is about how we got to where we are. That said, we do not recommend that you do exactly what we did. The first and most important part of the method we advocate is that you should become more self-aware so that the income streams you build reflect who you are and play to your specific strengths. However, we believe that the same basic strategies we used will also serve you well.

Dan's Bio

I've always been a natural explorer. I get bored quickly so pushing physical, personal and business boundaries livens things up. That buccaneering risk-taking attitude often gets me into trouble. When trying to embarrass me (which isn't difficult), my mom loves to tell the infamous "crib story".

It begins with a four-year old child who loved disobeying orders purely to see the consequences – however painful they might be. For reasons I cannot remember, my mom wanted me to leave my crib. I'm pretty sure I had no compelling reason to refuse the request, other than to assert my independence and test her reaction. I proudly exclaimed "you're not the boss of me." This declaration would have carried far more weight had the slit in my diaper not simultaneously fallen, revealing my majestic rear end to the world.

This is a good symbol of some of my toughest moments. I relieve boredom by pushing the boundaries and excitedly seeing what I can get away with. Sometimes, it works out and sometimes, it doesn't. As an apprentice lawyer at one of Canada's largest and most prestigious law firms, I had to complete 10 months of training (articling) before acquiring a license to practice law. Unlike my 15 articling peers, I had no intention of staying at the firm so I'd received a few other job offers, one of which required me to start before the end of articling. A small percentage of each firm's articling class chooses to leave, but to do so *before* the end of articling was extremely uncommon.

Even though I'd made a case to the lawyer licensing organization that I should be licensed anyway, there was no guarantee they'd agree. I left the firm not knowing if I'd be called to the bar. I was a bit scared. But I was compelled by seeing what would happen in such a novel situation.

Tony Robbins writes about the six fundamental human needs: Certainty, uncertainty, significance, connection/love, growth and contribution. He says that we all have these six needs but that we prioritize them differently. If this framework is at all valid, I know that the need for uncertainty is high on my list.

I've had enough experiences that showed me that you can break many of the rules we take for granted. You can create jobs for yourself and others out of thin air if you can convince an employer that it is worth their while. While in university, you can leave school for weeks on end – live in a different city, work somewhere else, or frankly do whatever you want instead of going to class. If you're an investor, you can experiment with asset classes beyond stocks, bonds and real estate.

This doesn't mean that we think you should do all those things or that if you try and you fail, there won't be consequences. It also doesn't mean that it is easy to ignore the rules and turn everything you touch to gold. It does mean, however, that there is tremendous value in thinking about pushing the boundaries. You learn nothing if you never challenge the rules, if only in your mind. I see life as a giant fun science experiment; each time I try something, I gather data and refine the experiment.

I took a big risk after my first year of law school. I was bored. So, there was nothing for it but to find a friend with the right mixture of insanity and reliability to join me on the *Mongol Rally*. It's a once-a-year charity car race starting in London and ending in Ulanbataar, Mongolia. How you get from point A, to point B, is up to you.

Our route took us through Russia, where things got hairy. In the middle of Siberia, our tiny Fiat had a life-changing encounter with a pothole. Its tiny engine, connected to the car by a flimsy piece of metal, would no longer accept our desperate pleas to start; the life-giving piece of metal was bent out of shape.

Our luck briefly appeared to improve when a Russian trucker pulled over, in response to my hitchhiking signal. He opened our hood. I said "auto kaput". He moved things around for a few minutes and then turned to me with an abrupt "Da," followed by an immediate return to his truck.

The second truck to pull over stayed longer. It was a Russian army truck. The three soldiers who lived in it managed to leverage our car's piece of metal back into place and the Fiat shuddered back to life. The soldiers demanded over 5000 rubles - about 80 USD today. My teammate, Mike, spent his last penny to participate in this mad adventure, so it was up to me to pay. The trouble was that I had no cash on me.

As is often the case in Russia, those who cannot pay must provide collateral. I was to be held in the back of their truck until we reached a bank machine (a bank - o - mat in Russian). Meanwhile, Mike would follow us in our quasi-functioning Fiat, this time carefully avoiding potholes. This arrangement lasted only 20 minutes until an impatient soldier pushed Mike out of the Fiat and drove our loyal chariot up a dirt road to be cruelly harvested for spare parts. The remaining soldiers, nevertheless, insisted on payment and since their AK-47 trigger fingers were itchy, I didn't argue.

With trepidation, I approached a bankomat in the middle of a swampy Siberian village. Everything smelled like death. Russian bank machines generally work because a society distrustful of credit cards is reliant on cash. But I found what, at the time, felt like the only malfunctioning bank machine in Russia. Luckily, the vodka I'd been drinking with the soldiers numbed me so that when I left the bankomat and slowly walked up to the 6'4 Russian soldier, carrying his AK-47, it was easy to say "bankomat kaput." A hint of a smile formed on his face and instead of reacting in anger as I feared he would, he abandoned us in the swampy village that smelt like death. And I've rarely felt so grateful. I remind myself of this moment whenever I hear myself complaining. And I think that moment is all the more memorable because I was in such an extreme, unlikely situation.

You don't have to be held hostage by the Russian army to gain perspective, but it sure helps! I cannot tell you to take the risks I've taken but I can tell you that if you do, there will be benefits you cannot predict in advance. The downsides are generally not that difficult to predict, so you can mitigate them.

Failing to mitigate predictable risks was my most significant early entrepreneurial failure. I left a comfortable six figure career to somehow make a living on my own mostly because I was too immature to obey a boss. I had no plan. There was no income stream I could rely on. Don't get me wrong – it wasn't as if I'd no ideas. But I conflated ideas with reality, and assumed the money would flow into my wallet as soon as I told the world that I was in business... how wrong I was. The money isn't in your pocket until the money is in your pocket, so I had not mitigated the most predictable risk of self-employment – not building a stable income stream in advance.

Luckily, there's a flip side to my instinct for take-no-prisoners risk-taking – while I can burn myself if the waters of uncertainty are too hot, my treading where others are afraid teaches me things others don't know. For example: My explorer's instinct led me to income-producing websites (online real estate) – an asset class of which few are aware. Fewer still are aware that there is a small but growing group of real estate agents and property managers for online real estate – so you can profit even if you've no clue how to buy or run such a website. This is one of a number of unconventional income streams I've learned about that make up my growing portfolio of multiple income streams. You'll learn about a number of unconventional possibilities later in this book. I hope they inspire you to think more creatively about your business and financial life.

I combine creativity with a deep interest in psychology. I constantly wonder why we do the things we do and how humans can best identify their natural gifts. When I first experimented with self-employment, I had a very ill-developed sense of my business strengths and weaknesses.

I was inspired by my experience working as an advisor to one of the investors on the Shark Tank TV show and, in retrospect, overconfidence. I thought I could do everything. But experience was a cruel teacher.

I felt I needed to be my own boss, but I had no idea what that would look like. I was not alone; most of us have no idea what our careers should look like so we let them happen to us. I believe that psychology can help us *design* our careers.

With no plan, I experienced crushing failure for the first time in my life. I judged myself by how much money I was making, and I was barely staying afloat as I whittled away time on poorly-paid freelance projects for which I was ill-suited: building excel models, drafting complex legal documents and writing an entire tour guide of Japan. I woke up one day with a gnawing pain in my stomach. Whenever my mind thought about the pain, it grew.

My doctor helped as did meditation and cognitive behavioural therapy. I studied psychometrics, the field of psychology which measures personality traits. And soon enough, I got the clarity I needed. I developed a "self-awareness cheat sheet" which reminds me of my gifts and where I need others to help me. I try to spend as much of every day as possible doing what I am good at and determining what others can do for me.

I now spend as much time as possible using my strengths and tasking others to cover for my weaknesses. It's a major reason why I've obtained the freedom I sought for so long. But there is still much more to do. I want to expand my business and help others build multiple income streams.

Mohit's Bio

I don't like labels, but if I had to describe myself, serial entrepreneur and investor would be the closest.

The backstory

I come from a city called Jodhpur, which is in the state of Rajasthan in India. In India, the tradition is to follow in your dad's footsteps. So, if your dad's a CPA, you need to become one too and if your dad's a lawyer, you become one, or at least try to. Sadly for me, my dad was a doctor and I was never remotely interested in becoming a doctor. So, the next best thing I could do was become an engineer.

I tried doing that but didn't quite like it, either. I tried to get into five different colleges. Finally, I made it to one of the top science institutes in India and studied Pharmacy there (computer science was way too competitive, and overrated too).

I had always known that I'd do my own thing and never do a regular nine to five job, but I didn't know what that one thing was. I still don't know. That one thing keeps changing every now and then as I move from one business to another.

It all started in high school when (like for a lot of other successful people I know) I read "Rich Dad Poor Dad" by Robert Kiyosaki. It was a defining moment in my life. Things started to make sense. The dream of passive income was too alluring to not chase.

My first "business" was fixing computers while I was in college. After that, I moved to trading stocks and mostly lost money, whatever little I'd made moonlighting during college. It was 2011 and it was graduation. I had two choices in front of me. I could either take up a corporate job or go do my Masters. I didn't like either, but still went ahead with the job. Though I got a job in a really cool startup (Zomato, now a unicorn), after a few months, it started to feel boring and unfulfilling.

It didn't take me long to realize that I wanted to spend my life doing something much more than sitting in an office doing boring stuff every day. I wanted to travel and live in other countries. I wanted to build *my own* business. I wanted to spend as much time as I wanted with my friends and family. I wanted to make more than $10k a year (which apparently is considered a good income in India). I realized that I couldn't do any of this while working for someone else. So, in mid-2012, I left my job having no idea what I would do next.

My first real business

While at my job, I had already started building websites in my spare time but was unable to make any money from them. Then I came across Flippa.com, which was a marketplace for established revenue generating websites. That was all I needed.

So, I went ahead and bought my first website for $2,500. I ran it for six months and then sold it for $12,000. Then I repeated it. The third time, I got scammed and there went all my previous earnings and gains. I was dejected and didn't know if I should continue buying websites. To tell you the truth, I was scared.

So, I moved on to another business. I started publishing books on Kindle. These were mostly short non-fiction books that helped the readers solve a pressing problem, whether becoming more productive or handling stress. I published over 12 books but they barely moved any numbers. At my best, I was doing about $300 a month from all the books combined. I realized I was a bad marketer.

So I dug into marketing and learned everything there was to learn about it. I read books, took up courses and even attended offline workshops about marketing, especially digital marketing.

And in 2014, I started my marketing agency Mixeron. It took a little while to fly, but fly it did and I started getting clients on a consistent basis. Soon I expanded and hired people to work for me as the work was getting too much for me to handle. I noticed that a majority of my clients wanted content writing services and so I launched a niche content agency Authority Writing and jacked up my prices, which people were more than happy to pay.

As I started making good money, I wanted my money to work for me. So I went back to Flippa and bought my first major website. It cost $10,000 which was a significant amount for me. But this time, I was not afraid of failing. I worked on the site and quadrupled the earnings within just three months.

It didn't take me long to buy more sites and by the end of 2015, I had a six-figure portfolio of websites. I currently have over 10 websites in my portfolio which my team manages for me.

As I was doing this for myself, a lot of people came to me and wanted to invest in websites and digital assets like I did. The only problem was they knew nothing about website investing. And that is how BlackBook Investments, my newest venture, was born. This taught me one thing; if there is a pressing need that you can fulfil, or a problem that you can solve, you will find no shortage of takers. In this case, I was helping people earn a higher ROI on their money.

Through BlackBook Investments, I help people invest in revenue-generating websites and earn a higher ROI than they could get from traditional investments such as real estate, stocks, bonds etc. Currently, BlackBook Investments manages over half a million dollars in assets.

The present

Currently, I run multiple businesses, which include, apart from the ones I already mentioned, a travel agency, a learning and education company, a furniture export company and my latest venture is a pizza restaurant. But the best part is that I run all these businesses from wherever I am in the world; yes, even the restaurant! I have also started angel investing in promising businesses (I hate the term startups).

I wanted to write this book with a clear purpose, which is to educate people about the various unconventional income streams that are available today to each one of us. I hope you will gain from my and Dan's experience.

Now that you have a sense of where we're coming from, let's talk about the different kinds of income streams you can create.

Passive, Active and Hybrid Income Streams

It's time to take stock of how much time and money you're willing to invest at the beginning of your multiple income streams journey. Those are by far the two most important resources you'll need to invest to create new income streams. The type of resources you're willing to invest affect the type of income streams you can create. We'll start this section with a discussion of three different types of income streams: passive, active and hybrid income streams.

Passive income streams are the stuff of internet legend - we challenge you to find a website about earning income online that does not promote the idea of passive income. Anyone with the slightest interest in early retirement fantasizes about the possibility of earning income while sleeping. Unfortunately, many people have deeply unrealistic expectations about earning passive income. Some people think that the road to passive income is very short. All they need to do is find the right idea and voila, passive income automatically flows into your bank account. To others, passive income is a lie foisted on the Internet's most gullible to rob them of their hard-earned savings. Our experience is that both opinions are misinformed.

Passive income does not grow on trees nor will it appear after you express some especially passionate affirmations to the mother Earth goddess – you will have to work for it, though passive income streams are not the most labor-intensive type of income stream. Contrary to some beliefs, passive income *is a real thing*. We can both confirm that. A passive income stream need not be some extremely fancy online business that only two people know anything about - it can be as simple as owning a stock, though of course, there are passive income streams that are far more unconventional. But for the time being, let's start with stocks in publicly traded companies.

If you've purchased shares of a publicly traded company, you can earn a return on your investment in two ways:

1. A capital gain, if you sell the stock at a higher price than the purchase price. This is equal to the

difference between the price at the time of sale and the purchase price.

2. A dividend, if the company chooses to pay shareholders a percentage of profits.

In either case, after you own the shares, there's very little work involved for you to earn income; no work whatsoever, if we're talking about dividends. Keep in mind the two major resources you can invest to create an income stream: time and money. Here, there's no requirement for you to invest time – the hallmark of a passive income stream. If the company required shareholders to show up to work the day after purchase, that would change things. And indeed, many employees are rewarded with stock in addition to cash compensation – but they must show up to work because they're employees, not because they're stockholders.

By contrast, an active income stream requires you to invest more time than money. You've probably heard of the company Uber, which has revolutionized the taxi industry. For those that are unaware, Uber enables ordinary people to serve as taxi drivers. The app allows users to hail nearby cabs and determine how long it will take for a cab to arrive, how expensive the ride will be and the quality of service they are likely to receive (based on a 5-star rating system for drivers and passengers).

If you want to drive for Uber, you must give Uber your time. They do not want your money. This is about as extreme an active income stream as you can find; you are not earning anything when you are not driving. Any kind of freelancer who trades his or her time for money has an active income stream. Most employees can think of their jobs as *active income streams*, as their employers require them to trade their time for money.

Your first reaction might be that passive income streams are *better* than active income streams. But this isn't necessarily the case, nor is it productive thinking when you keep in mind that not everyone is well-positioned to earn passive income. Some people like the work they do, as crazy as that sounds to people who dislike their work. If you enjoy providing your labor, you might enjoy building a relevant active income stream. Even if you're lazy and dislike the work you do or could most easily do to earn revenue, you have to be practical; if you don't have much money, it will be very difficult to build a passive income stream.

Generally speaking, younger people are more likely to have time, rather than money, at their disposal. Older folks are more likely to have the money for passive income streams. But of course, there are plenty of exceptions. Take stock of your reserves in time and money and keep them in mind when deciding which income streams to experiment with.

One final point to understand with respect to passive and active income streams: not every income stream fits neatly into one of the two categories. That's why we think of income streams on a spectrum instead of a dichotomy. No income stream is strictly passive or active. Some income streams are hard to classify as more on the active or passive side of the spectrum so we call them *hybrid* income streams.

For example: building an online coaching business requires more time than money at the beginning. Things change as time goes on: scaling the business requires far more paid advertising and less labor as you create systems like autoresponders or you can just hire the right people to do the work for you. If an income stream requires both money and time, you'll need to evaluate when it requires time and when it requires money so that you can decide whether you're likely to be able to invest the right resource at the right time. That's what matters.

In the third chapter, we will dive deeply into 10 income stream ideas. While reading it, we suggest keeping in mind your ideal combination of active and passive income streams. We will discuss a variety of active, passive and hybrid income stream ideas. Now that we know the types of income streams we can create and the resources each one requires, how do we start creating a new income stream?

The Multiple Income Streams Method (MIS Method)

Blueprints are extremely useful in the age of overwhelm because there is no shortage of information, yet it's hard to know where to start any significant project. A good blueprint cuts through the seemingly endless noise and leaves us with a crystal-clear path to our goal. The precise nature of your path to successfully creating multiple income streams will vary - there are as many paths as people, and each income stream requires different skills. However, we've noticed that some common strategies, if followed in the right order, are extremely effective.

We believe everyone should begin by getting super clear on the unique gifts they bring to the table. This will start out as a businesslike appraisal of your business skills but will be even more valuable in business and in life if your inquiry is even broader. You will get the most juice if you ask yourself harder questions about why you are doing what you are doing, and why you want to do what you want to do. The more you know yourself, the better your decisions will be when it comes to deciding which income streams to pursue and how best to pursue them. As of November 2016, there are a ton of unconventional income stream opportunities, as you will discover if you read this book cover to cover. Each of the income streams we discuss is a proven approach but that does not mean YOU are well-suited to implement each one? Dan can give you a whole bunch of examples of great business ideas he attempted to implement, but either the ideas or the ways in which he tried to implement them were ill-suited to his skill set. So, everything starts with you. You will learn a lot about yourself through the exercises in Chapter 2 so do not skip this section even if you're tempted to do so.

Once you know you, Chapter 3 will expose you to a range of unconventional income stream ideas. We are both attracted to unconventional ideas for a number of reasons. A big one is that many people are competing to implement more conventional ideas. It's always good to feel ahead of the curve but even better to *actually be* ahead of the curve.

For all our frustrations with 2017's multitude of distractions like social media, smart phones and notifications, we too often forget the upsides. Politicians and social critics whine and whinge about a lack of economic opportunity but there has never been more *unconventional* opportunities available to those that are willing to explore. Investors, traders and the TV channels they watch like CNBC talk about stocks, bonds and real estate. We don't think they are a waste of time but we advocate exploring other possibilities as well, analyzing what the data tells us and making the best choices for us – which is not a conversation enough of us are having.

In Chapter 4, we'll discuss productivity. How productive do you think you are? Probably more than you actually are. We've given you rare information about self-awareness and psychology and how it connects to a multitude of rare income stream opportunities so it would be a great shame if you did nothing with that information. Most of us like to think of ourselves as action takers, but the reality is that many of us do not put our money where our mouth is. How often have you heard yourself say, "I want to do that but I don't have time" or "I should do that but for whatever reason I haven't done it yet... I'll get to it later". It doesn't get much more human... We each have a set of productivity weaknesses. Our view is that these are nothing to be ashamed of but we should work to be more productive.

It starts with self-awareness so we can catch unproductive actions and thought patterns. Once we've acknowledged them, we can implement productivity systems designed to diminish them. We can build new productive thought patterns and systems to keep ourselves on track. We've been amazed in our own lives at how much more productive we've become as a result of following this advice. There's nothing special about us so when it comes to this section, odds are that the same approach will work for you. So, without further ado, let's move on to Chapter 2 and discuss self-awareness.

Self-Awareness

It used to be that most of the self-help books ignored this subject. Luckily, things are changing – and that's for good reason. Self-awareness is, in our view, the single most important quality you need to create multiple income streams or do anything entrepreneurial. We can give you all the good ideas in the world, but if those ideas are not a match for you... if they do not fit you like a glove, you won't execute, or you won't execute well. Make no mistake – ideas matter. But ideas are a necessary but not sufficient condition for success. You absolutely 100% need to know what you're good at before anything else.

More and more of the how-to content for entrepreneurs features great information about the importance of mindset. We used to skip those steps for the same reason that many people skip those steps: they think it's a waste of time when they could be learning the tactics that more obviously produce results. Social media and the rise of the distraction culture has trained us to seek quick fixes; our impatience challenges us to do the work that requires deeper reflection but yields deeper truths.

Even those influencers who preach self-awareness often say that there is no system or concrete checklist of things you can do to guarantee self-awareness. As an example, read this excerpt from a Larry King interview of influencer Gary Vaynerchuk, on entrepreneurship:

> Larry King: "You're big on self-awareness, right?"
>
> Gary Vaynerchuk: "Huge."
>
> Larry: "How does one get to be… self-aware?"
>
> Gary: "I don't know."
>
> Larry: "So how do you teach it?"
>
> Gary: "I don't know… but I know it's damn important."

They rightly say that self-awareness cannot be learned as quickly as more concrete business skills like discounted cash flow analysis. But you would be wrong to conclude that <u>there are not proven approaches you can use to significantly increase your self-awareness.</u> In this chapter, we will give you six suggestions. You need not nor likely have the time to experiment with all of them. But odds are that even just a couple will pay huge dividends for the rest of your life.

Self-Awareness Tool #1: Myers-Briggs

This test is the best-known psychological profiling system in the world. Two psychologists developed it in the 1940s. American women entered the workforce in World War 2 for the first time, so the test was introduced to help them figure out what made them tick and what kind of work they could do. You've probably taken the test yourself so you may have an opinion about its usefulness. It is extremely hard to come up with a theory of personality so while this test is imperfect, we feel its creators deserve great respect for giving it a shot.

This is because who we are matters a great deal. It is hard to argue that our natural hardwiring does not play a huge role in shaping who we are and thus what value we can create in the world. We are influenced by other factors like our environment and upbringing but many of us must accept that we will never be a great power forward in the NBA (at 5'10 and a half and 140 pounds, this is a cruel realization for Dan). Myers-Briggs wrestles with the question of who we are *relative to others.* None of us are good at everything and since we need to build teams in business, or choose what to focus on if you're a solopreneur, we must understand our hardwiring and that of those around us.

For those that are not Myers-Briggs aficionados, here's the basic version of how it works:

People can be categorized into one of 16 personalities, based on their placement on four personality trait spectra:

1. Introversion/Extroversion
2. Intuition/Sensing
3. Thinking/Feeling
4. Judging/Perceiving

Introversion/Extroversion

Many people think the first spectrum relates to whether you're socially skilled or not. There's a very common stereotype about introverts: they're usually awkward conversationalists. But this isn't necessarily the case. Some introverts are more socially skilled than some extroverts.

This dichotomy is about whether you gain or lose energy from social interaction. Do you become bored if you only go out three or four times per week? Does conversation energize you or do you look at conversation as draining? If you're not sure, you could be an ambivert; many people are halfway between the two extremes.

Intuition/Sensing

This is about how we process the information we receive from the world around us. Intuitive people are imaginative, theoretical, big picture-thinkers. Their intuition focuses them on the future – what will their lives be like 10 years from now? This can lead them to ignore the past or, more importantly, what is going on right now. Do you know people who seek novelty so much that they easily become bored with perfectly good lives? We do – because we're both intuitives! It's a common trait among entrepreneurs though only about 25% of the North American population is intuitive.

There's a common stereotype that women tend to be more intuitive than men. You've probably heard the expression "women's intuition." For your information, the data is inconclusive on whether women are likely to be more intuitive than men.

Intuitives are more likely to come up with unconventional ideas but are less likely to be the practical implementers of those ideas. They may be able to see the world in a different way, but they are usually less able to appreciate the practical steps necessary to implement their visions. Think Steve Jobs. They are more interested in possibilities than actualities.

Sensors, on the other hand, are concrete, practical, detail-focused and present-oriented people. It's probably a good thing that 75% of North Americans are sensors. Otherwise, we're not sure anything would ever get done! Sensors like to break tasks down into step-by-step processes. They spend less time stuck in their heads and more time seeing the world around them.

Thinking/Feeling

This is about decision-making. Do you tend to make decisions with your heart or your head? Feelers prioritize relationships over their competitive instincts. They are generally more sensitive and are affected by others' discomfort. Feelers may not know they are feelers, particularly if they are young and have spent a lifetime in an education system that does not emotionally engage them. They may *believe* they make decisions for logical reasons as it is easy to come up with a seemingly rational justification for any decision. But the more extreme the feeler, the less likely they are to decide based on a logical framework. A great example is that sales studies strongly suggest that buyers typically do not make rational decisions but find post-purchase ways to rationalize their decisions.[3]

The stereotypical thinker is more distant from events, thus she or he finds it easier to view events through a logical

---

[3] https://thesalesblog.com/2012/09/25/buyers-make-emotional-decisions-and-justify-them-later/

prism. Extreme thinkers are frequently surprised by others' illogical decisions, as they lack empathy. Because they prioritize efficiency over relationships, they are typically more competitive than feelers. Think Steve Jobs or Margaret Thatcher.

Judging/Perceiving

Judging types are more common than perceivers. They tend to view the world in a structured way so when they are given a task, they create to-do lists and a schedule so they can plan when to accomplish each item on the to-do list. They prefer to schedule necessary activities in advance, as much as possible. They narrowly focus on one or a small number of tasks. They look for certainty, safety and stability. This makes them generally effective in conventional, hierarchical contexts like medicine, law, education and government. It can make them hostile to unconventional ideas or just less interested in them. They are better executors than creators.

Perceivers are less conformist and judgmental; they are open to exploring more unconventional ideas, risking judgment. Bursts of energy motivate them to work, though they can often lose interest in a project as they don't have the judger's consistent energy level. They see spontaneity as a gift – the ability to learn and explore at one's own pace is priceless. They can be extremely unwilling to take orders and so tend to do less well in the hierarchical organizations that judgers build and maintain. Perceivers may see judgers as inflexible and stuck in old ways.

Since this test is often self-assessed, you should use some of the other self-awareness tools we give you to confirm its findings. You can also do multiple versions of the test. Here are two slightly different versions:

1. Quistic – This is a traditional version. There are 72 'yes' or 'no' questions. It takes about 5 minutes.
2. 16Personalities – This is a modified version. There are 70 agree/disagree spectrum questions. It takes about 10 minutes. It includes a fifth, less significant trait pairing.

This exercise is valuable for so many reasons but let us highlight one big one for you: No type is better than any other type but each type has strengths and weaknesses. Especially if you're an extreme example of your type, odds are that you will be more successful in everything you do if you're aware of those strengths and weaknesses. Then you can design systems to mitigate the risks caused by your weaknesses.

For example, Dan's an ENFP. He is a master at creating unconventional ideas but he is not the world's greatest implementer. Sometimes he works on a small project that he must do himself – because it is too small to bring in a team. In these situations, he <u>has</u> to do the work even though a J is much more suited to doing the work! This is particularly challenging if the work involves repetitive tasks that don't engage his creative mind. When confronted with work of that nature, he would much rather do something else. Because he is always working on lots of different projects, he will happily work on something he prefers. He has designed productivity systems to solve this problem.

More about those in the productivity section of the book but suffice to say, he wouldn't have known he needed to do this if it wasn't for Myers-Briggs.

Self-Awareness Tool #2: Meditation

Have you tried meditating? What was your experience like? Did you stick with it? Perhaps you do it every day or perhaps you liked it but gave up the habit and constantly tell yourself I should go back to meditating. Regardless of your prior experience, meditation can help you now and in the future, if you want more self-awareness.

What is meditation doing in a book about entrepreneurship? Dan is often asked the same question by the students in his *Entrepreneurship* class at McGill University, in which meditation is on the syllabus. The answer is that the ups and downs in any business can harshly affect our mental health. Many entrepreneurs know that something is amiss but they can't put their finger on it. This roller coaster ride is worsened by a poorly controlled mind. Even if you struggle to control your mind, you will gain some peace just by being more aware of its constant barrage of thoughts.

For those who see meditation as solely the domain of woo-woo spiritual types, know that science is showing that meditation can boost focus and productivity, reduce stress and anxiety, improve sleep quality and aid in creative problem-solving. What's not to like?

We're not scientists so this is not a comprehensive chapter on all the benefits of meditation so we're going to focus on just one benefit: self-awareness. Do you have a voice in your head? It's okay to admit if you do. You're not Joan of Arc so you're not going to be tried for heresy by the English and burned at the stake. The truth is that we all have a voice in our head. Exactly where that voice comes from is a tricky question. Luckily, we do not need to know the answer to know that that voice is not always helpful.

If you listen to that voice carefully you may be astonished to know how negative it is. It is an unending source of worry. It affects some of us more than others but we all benefit if we are aware of what it is saying and if we don't accept everything as gospel. Take a moment now and close your door, turn off the light and set your smartphone timer to five minutes. Spend the next five minutes watching the voice. After your alarm clock wakes you up, grab a piece of paper or a Word document and write down some of the thoughts you heard. Please do not continue reading until you've completed this short exercise.

Notice anything remarkable? We're willing to bet at least a few of the thoughts were downright crazy. No, this doesn't mean that you're destined to spend the next 10 years of your life in an insane asylum. It does mean that you are a human being, and part of the human condition is that this voice unendingly bombards us with inaccurate thoughts. The real tragedy is when we are so unaware of this that we uncritically accept everything we are told. You may have heard the quotation that the mind is a great servant but a terrible master. Now you know why.

The voice is even more negative than usual when you feel as if nothing is going well. We all go through tough times and we don't need a crazy voice making them worse. Odds are that this has happened to you many times in the past and will continue to happen. In his excellent commencement speech to the graduates of Kenyon

College, David Foster Wallace analysed the banal statement that a liberal arts education is about teaching you how to think. In his view, this means being aware of your inner voice and how much pain it can cause you. He talks about the average adult day that the graduates are soon to experience, and how unawareness of the inner voice is a problem:

"You get up in the morning, go to your challenging job, and you work hard for nine or ten hours, and at the end of the day you're tired, and you're stressed out, and all you want is to go home and have a good supper and maybe unwind for a couple of hours and then hit the rack early because you have to get up the next day and do it all again. But then you remember there's no food at home-you haven't had time to shop this week, because of your challenging job-and so now after work, you have to get in your car and drive to the supermarket. It's the end of the workday, and the traffic's very bad, so getting to the store takes way longer than it should, and when you finally get to the supermarket, it is very crowded, because of course it's the time of day when all the other people with jobs also try to squeeze in some grocery shopping, and the store's hideously, fluorescently lit, and infused with soul-killing Muzak or corporate pop, and it's pretty much the last place you want to be, but you can't just get in and quickly out. You have to wander all over the huge, over lit store's crowded aisles to find the stuff you want, and you have to maneuver your junky cart through all these other tired, hurried people with carts, and of course there are also the glacially slow old people and the spacey people and the ADHD kids who all block the aisle and you have to grit your teeth and try to be polite as you ask them to let you by, and eventually, finally, you get all your supper supplies, except now it turns out there aren't enough checkout lanes open even though it's the end-of-the-day rush, so the checkout line is incredibly long, which is stupid and infuriating, but you can't take your fury out on the frantic lady working the register.

Anyway, you finally get to the front of the checkout line, and pay for your food, and wait to get your check or card authenticated by a machine, and then get told to "Have a nice day" in a voice that is the absolute voice of death, and then you have to take your creepy flimsy plastic bags of groceries in your cart through the crowded, bumpy, littery parking lot, and try to load the bags in your car in such a way that everything doesn't fall out of the bags and roll around in the trunk on the way home, and then you have to drive all the way home through slow, heavy, SUV-intensive rush-hour traffic, et cetera, et cetera.

The point is that petty, frustrating crap like this is exactly where the work of choosing comes in. Because the traffic jams and crowded aisles and long checkout lines give me time to think, and if I don't make a conscious decision about how to think and what to pay attention to, I'm going to be pissed and miserable every time I have to food shop, because my natural default-setting is the certainty that situations like this are really all about me, about my hungriness and my fatigue and my desire to just get home, and it's going to seem, for all the world, like everybody else is just in my way, and who are all these people in my way? And look at how repulsive most of them are and how stupid and cow-like and dead-eyed and nonhuman they seem here in the checkout line, or at how annoying and rude it is that people are talking loudly on cell phones in the middle of the line, and look at how deeply unfair this is: I've worked really hard all day and I'm starved and tired and I can't even get home to eat and unwind because of all these stupid goddamn people."[4]

Being aware of the voice in your head is the first step – because it's the voice in your head that complains about being stuck in the check-out line, in traffic, and in what appears to be a meaningless, vapid existence. But – and this is easier said than done – *you can choose what to think*:

"But most days, if you're aware enough to give yourself a choice, you can choose to look differently at this fat, dead-eyed, over-made-lady who just screamed at her little child in the checkout line. Maybe she's not usually like this; maybe she's been up three straight nights holding the hand of her husband who's dying of bone cancer, or maybe this very lady is the low-wage clerk at the DMV who just yesterday helped your spouse resolve a nightmarish red-

---

[4] *Foster Wallace, David*. This is Water. Commencement Speech.

tape problem through some small act of bureaucratic kindness. Of course, none of this is likely, but is's also not impossible. It just depends on what you want to consider. If you're automatically sure that you know what reality is and who and what is really – if you want to operate on your default-setting then you, like me, will not consider possibilities that aren't pointless and annoying. But if you've really learned how to think, how to pay attention, then you will know you have other options. It will actually be within your power to experience a crowded, loud, slow, consumer hell-type situation as not only meaningful but sacred, on fire with the same force that lit the stars: compassion, love, the sub-surface unity of all things. Not that that mystical stuff's necessarily true: The only thing that's capital-T True is that you get to *decide* how you're going to try to see it. You get to consciously decide what has meaning and what doesn't. You get to decide what to worship."[5]

---

[5] *Foster Wallace, David*. This is Water. Commencement Speech.

How do you exercise that choice? David Foster Wallace did not discuss it in *This is Water*, but in our view, meditation is a great approach. Meditation trains you to pay attention. It does this in a very simple way: by practising paying attention.

If you spend 10 minutes in a dark room (so that there is no sensory stimulation), and focus on one image, word, concept or mantra, you will be practising the all-important art of attention. This may seem so simple that it is hard to understand what all the fuss is about. It may be equally hard to understand how this is so impactful. Let's clear up both of those misconceptions.

That this is simple does not mean that it is easy to do day in and day out. In the age of distraction, where excitement and stimulation are around every corner, the simplest possible activity can seem like the most boring. One of the many benefits of meditation is that it prepares us for some of life's most trying moments, where there is no substitute for honest to goodness hard work. Do you feel like technology makes it harder for you to do simple but repetitive tasks? Meditation is part of the antidote.

If you want to build multiple income streams, you're going to need a lot of get up and go. At the beginning, inspired by an idea, it will be easier to get to work. But once the idea's initial sexy charms wear off, you're left with something far more ordinary - you're left with the need to roll up your sleeves and to actually get shit done. If you're not as productive as you'd like, particularly when it comes to repetitive work, we recommend you give meditation a shot.

So now that you understand what it means to pay attention and appreciate the value of practising attention, what do you do to practice attention? It's as simple as this:

1. As described earlier, pick a couple of words (it can be any small number of words) or a memorable image.
2. Set your smart phone alarm for five minutes.
3. Close your door, turn off the lights, and watch your thoughts.

4. Your thoughts will drift away from your focus. That's okay. When you catch your thoughts drifting away from your focus, gently return.
5. After the alarm wakes you, write the thoughts you remember on a piece of paper.
6. And, voilà, you have an age-old, time-tested self-awareness technique.

Depending on what's happening in your life, the nature of the thoughts will change. What will not change is that you have the thoughts. Do not judge them. Know that they will be there and that they are part of you but that they should not rule you. The more you can pay attention to those thoughts, the more you will understand why you have done the things you have done in the past. And when it comes to the present and the future, you will start to notice more distance between your thoughts and actions.

The true you will emerge and it will be a beautiful thing.

Self-Awareness Tool #3: Journaling

Do you feel as if life is passing you by? Does it seem like time is moving more quickly than it used to when you were a child? If someone asked you what the highlights were of your life in the last month, would it be easy to come up with an answer? If you appreciated our last section on meditation, you no doubt appreciate the value of slowing life down. Your experiences are that much richer when you can stop to reflect. The simple act of looking at the autumn leaves when you walk the streets instead of being consumed in the endless madness of your thoughts may leave you breathless with wonder, if you've never done it before.

Journaling is a great approach to force yourself to stop and reflect on a regular basis. Some of our most successful corporate and entrepreneurial friends have a monthly journaling habit. This enables them to take stock on a regular basis. You may do things that you don't even know you're doing. Or, you may be fully aware of everything you're doing without stopping to appreciate it.

Understanding the good and the bad of what you do is vital to living a more meaningful life.

Dan recently started a new journal. Unlike most of the people we know who have a private journal, he sends his to the people he cares about most. Some people post deeply personal writing on Facebook. Dan did not do so because, like most of the rest of us, he has many Facebook friends who he is not in frequent touch with. Email, as anonymous as it may sometimes seem, is a far more personal choice than Facebook. The recipients of the emails are grateful to be included as the world can often seem impersonal, and so for someone to take the time to reach out and connect in such a personal fashion is extremely rare. It's like sending an old-fashioned hand written note. Dan's journal includes three sections: a personal section, a business section, and a top 10 content list. The final item directly adds value to readers' lives so it's one more reason to read the journal.

Whether your journal is public, semi-public, or private, if you are honest with yourself or others, you will be amazed at the results. Journaling can be as simple as sitting down with your notebook each day and writing whatever comes to mind. It can be just 100 words or it can be page after page. It's up to you. Two good places you can start are: The Self Journal and Julia Cameron's Morning Pages. If you're looking for motivation to experiment with this, always remember that you are the center of your own universe; no one matters more to you than you, so what are you waiting for? Journal away!

Self-Awareness Tool #4: Long Walks

If you're a reader bored with what seems like an unending parade of spiritual/woo woo self-awareness concepts, you're in luck. Our next tool is as old-fashioned as it gets. We appreciate the meaning of the expression "different strokes for different folks" because we know that some readers will not want to experiment with something totally new and unfamiliar. Could there be anything more familiar than a good, old-fashioned, constitutional?

The long walk may not seem like anything special. Many of us, without thinking about it, do it every day. Like meditation, a long walk is a great opportunity to be alone with our thoughts. Those don't come around very often in the age of distraction. Like meditation, when we are alone with our thoughts, we are forced to confront them. This means we will be confronted with the good and the bad - the stuff of self-awareness.[6]

---

[6] https://designschool.canva.com/blog/taking-long-walks/

The great thing about the long walk is that there's a good chance it's already part of your daily routine and you won't need to change anything other than the length and frequency of your walks. If you want to quicken the process, try to watch your thoughts as you're walking. Like with meditation, you can write your thoughts down afterwards. You can also keep track of them in a journal and watch how your thoughts change over time.

How many great works of literature mention long walks? Particularly long walks in the woods? If it isn't a horror novel in which the main character is assaulted by a zombie in the forest, odds are the main character uses walks as an opportunity for reflection. Literature is so often a reflection of human nature; an opportunity to access centuries of human experience and harness it to improve your own life. There's a reason long walks appear so frequently in literature. We highly recommend you add them to your daily routine. If not for self-awareness, do it for those frustrating moments when writer's block or some other bizarre, seemingly immovable barrier, blocks your way. A nice long walk may be just what you needed. For us, it often hits the spot.

Self-Awareness Tool #5: Asking Others

To this point, all the self-awareness tools we've discussed require a deep inner journey into the soul. They are introverted self-awareness techniques. Self-awareness is not just a journey for you; it is a journey for anyone around you. And I'm not just talking about other people's self-awareness – I'm talking about your own. The company you keep matters a great deal and one of the most powerful things friends can do for one another is to tell the truth even when it hurts – especially when it hurts.

There is so much to be gained by asking your friends what they think about you, something you've done, or something you are thinking about doing. Before you do this, be sure that your skin is sufficiently thick. If they know your skin is insufficiently thick, then they will hold back. And if they don't know, but you know, you won't be able to use the good advice you get.

There are some things you can do to thicken your skin. Warning: the following suggestions are not for the faint of heart. But if you appreciate the expression that you should do the things you fear; you won't think we're crazy. Go to the busiest square in your city and hand out brochures or even better, stop passersby and ask them what their first impressions of you are. Engage them in conversation. As you might expect, you will face plenty of rejection. You will become accustomed to the punch in the gut and you will grow to fear it less and less. In time, you will no longer fear rejection and when you no longer fear rejection or at least fear it less then you once did, you will be able to test new income stream ideas with far more confidence… More on that later.

Next, ask your friends some crucial questions. Have you wondered what they think about major issues in your life? You must control your instincts to judge their answers harshly, for that too, is one reason why they are unlikely to be truly honest with you. Try to anticipate in advance all the reasons why they may not be fully honest with you. Tell them that the more honest they can be, the more you will learn, and the stronger you will become. We don't advocate that you learn 20 harsh truths all at once – perhaps a few, one at a time, is enough as you're going to want to reflect deeply on what you learn. You may wish to use some of the other self-awareness tools to do so – meditation, journaling and long walks are all great candidates. It's also a great gesture to your friends to offer to repay the favor, for those who are interested.

To ensure that you get the most out of the difficult conversations, we suggest you prepare a list of questions in advance. You can suggest that your friends do the same if you would like to repay the favour. You can take note of what they say in your first couple of conversations and use what you learn to come up with even stronger questions for subsequent conversations.

Self-Awareness Tool #6: Cognitive Behavioral Therapy

Neither of us are therapists but we've benefited from their work. Since we're not therapists, we won't directly recommend one particular type of therapy but we will tell you what worked for us: cognitive behavioural therapy.

Let's start off with the Wikipedia definition: "[CBT] is the most widely used evidence-based practice for treating mental disorders.[3] Guided by empirical research, CBT focuses on the development of personal coping strategies that target solving current problems and changing unhelpful patterns in cognitions (e.g., thoughts, beliefs, and attitudes), behaviors, and emotional regulation.[2][4] It was originally designed to treat depression, and is now used for a number of mental health conditions."

Even those of us who have no obvious mental disorders can benefit from CBT. This is because we're all a little bit crazy and neurotic. In the meditation section, we discussed the value of developing awareness of your thoughts because awareness of your thoughts will diminish the likelihood that your thoughts, especially the deeply negative ones, will rule you. Meditation makes you aware of your negative thought patterns through deep inner work whereas CBT makes you aware of your negative thought patterns through conversation with a therapist.

For many people, this process is faster. It also has the advantage of, if not objectivity, someone else's external perspective. If you are the woman or man in the arena, you are not always best-positioned to objectively judge which of your thoughts are helpful and harmful. An experienced therapist can help you get to the bottom of what is happening in your mind.

Each of these self-awareness tools can be extremely useful on its own. Used in conjunction with others, you will be amazed at the results. Do not fear what you will learn for even the harshest possible truths can set you free if you're ready for them. We acknowledge that it's not easy to hear those challenging truths and so you must trust your friends and your soul with the task of deciding what you are truly ready for. It goes without saying that since we are not doctors or therapists, we strongly recommend that you consult a qualified professional if you've any doubt about what might happen if you use these tools. They will be able to tell you what to do. But be sure that you take the task of self-awareness seriously, for you must learn more about yourself if you want to build new and multiple income streams. Do not skip this section because of fear about what you might discover or impatience. Until you take the time to complete some of these exercises, you will not know what you're ready for.

Following-Up: A Self-Awareness Cheat Sheet

There's a great way to keep track of everything you've learned in this chapter: A self-awareness cheat sheet. Dan keeps his in a PDF form and refers to it in times of trouble or when thinking about a new income stream idea. If you're anything like him, there's a good chance you'll forget what you've learned, even if you realized it was super-important at the time!

You can design your self-awareness cheat sheet the way you want but here's a simple one page version of Dan's:

Self-Awareness Cheat Sheet

MBTI/16 Personalities Profile: ENFP

"(do not like to be) beset by administrative tasks and routine maintenance."

"ENFPs' self-esteem is dependent on their ability to come up with original solutions, and they need to know that they have the freedom to be innovative."

"ENFPs have strong people skills."

Plum Profile: "Your Talent for being a Power House is in the top 5% of the workforce. You have an extraordinary proficiency for driving complex projects to completion and using political savvy to get things done."

"Exceptionally well suited to positions that require identifying and understanding the motivations and feelings of people."

You have a proficiency for generating creative ideas, out-of-the-box solutions to problems and entrepreneurship."

Strengths:

Extroversion

Creativity

Ambitious

Weaknesses:

Easily bored

Dislike mundane, everyday tasks

Independent to a fault

Skills:

Creating new business ideas

Resolving conflicts

Building teams

Things to Remember:

1. Meditate every day for at least 10 minutes.
2. Talk to 10 friends to learn their perspectives re my strengths and weaknesses
3. Do not take on projects that are not a fit for my strengths or, at minimum, find someone who can help who makes up for my weaknesses.

The Culmination of your Self-Awareness Efforts: The Unique Ability Concept

As evidence that all this hard work is worthwhile, we suggest you add a final element to your self-awareness cheat sheet: Your *unique ability*. This is a concept discussed in a great book of the same name by Catherine Nomura and Julia Waller. They argue that we all have a unique ability that is a major secret to our success if we use it. Our unique ability is:

1. A natural talent – something we do almost unconsciously
2. Something we love doing
3. Something that energizes us
4. An ability that is suited to lifetime improvement

The authors suggest thinking of your unique ability in three steps. Dan's unique ability is:

1. A buccaneering, risk-taking creativity that empowers me to discover unconventional ideas,

2. An intuitive sense of how to apply those ideas in other's lives,
3. And a love of teaching those ideas and coaching others to implement them.

Now it's your turn. What is your unique ability? Struggling to figure it out? There are a few things you can do. If you've completed your self-awareness cheat sheet, you can use it for inspiration. The authors suggest asking friends, as we discussed in an earlier section of this chapter. Try also to think about the successes of which you're most proud or the types of successes that you most commonly achieve. There will likely be clues there.

Once we know our unique ability, our goal should be to use it as much as possible. It may seem obvious in retrospect that we should do what we are best at but ask yourself, are you super clear on it? If not, this framework is a helpful way to achieve that monumentally important goal. You can use the concept in job interviews so that you are super straightforward with potential employers about what you're really good at and you can use it to build new income streams. You do this by breaking down each potential income stream into its constituent elements, in advance, and thinking through whether your unique ability is suited to most of the work and, for those elements for which it is unsuitable, determining whether they are easily outsourced. To make that calculation, you're going to need some income stream ideas. So, let's not keep you waiting any longer. We'll see you in the next chapter.

12 Creative Income Stream Ideas and how to Raise Money for Them

There are so many more good ideas than there used to be and it is easier than ever to learn about them. Globalization. The Internet. You know the story. While so many people squander their valuable time whining and whingeing about job losses, outsourcing and the rapid pace of technological change, you can spend your time deciding which ideas are right for you. There is little doubt that the new economic world will be tougher for some people than others. But since it doesn't seem like there's any prospect of things slowing down, even if things haven't gone well for you, the most rational response is to figure out something that *can* work for you. Behold 10 creative income stream ideas. Each one may or may not be right for you. We hope you enjoy them or get some inspiration to come up with new ideas if you don't absolutely love these brilliant ideas.

Niche Websites

We're going to start you off with an absolute barnburner. More and more people are buying websites that generate income for them. And many of these people don't know anything about coding, web development, programming and in some extreme cases, barely understand what the Internet is. Don't believe us? How is this possible? We'll explain.

The best way to get started is with niche websites. A niche website focuses on one very specific interest. It hosts good content relating to that interest, shows relevant advertisements and markets goods and services that are of interest to people who share that interest. An example: Smart watches. Not a subject that interests everyone. But the people who care about smart watches really care about smart watches. There are smart watch websites that update people on developments in the smartwatch industry and review and promote cool new smart watches. The owners of niche websites can promote their own offers or other people's offers in exchange for a commission. The most important key to all of this is to draw as many eyeballs as possible to your site. The larger the audience, the more products and services the site will sell and the more interested advertisers will be in paying you.

Here's another way to think about niche websites: Think of them as online real estate – as opposed to ordinary real estate. If you're an ordinary real estate investor, you're hoping to take advantage of one or both of these wealth-building tools:

1. Capital gains (the real estate increases in value and so you can sell it for a profit) or
2. Dividends (you earn cash flow from residential or commercial tenants – you can re-invest the cash flow to pay off your mortgage or use it for any other purpose you can think of).

Real estate investors work hard. If they want to boost their capital gain, they can make improvements to the property and if they want more dividend income, they will need to secure and manage tenants. In many instances, especially if the commercial or residential property is in a lower income neighbourhood, the renters have less incentive to look after the property than the owner. But if the owner doesn't live there and even if the owner does live there, odds are that the renters spend more time at the property. So, there is a real risk that tenants will cause problems of all kinds.

To buy real estate in the first place, most investors must use a real estate agent. Managing improvements or tenants takes a lot of time and energy and since most real estate investors are trying to create as passive an income stream as possible, they do not want to do the work themselves. So, they hire real estate agents to help acquire properties and property managers to manage the properties. The downside is that this cuts into their margins – they need to pay the property managers and real estate agents. Make sense? Let's compare this state of affairs with the similar but different world of online real estate.

In the online real estate world, there are no tenants so you don't have to worry about the toilets getting clogged. It is possible that hackers may rear their ugly heads but this is a highly unlikely scenario. But like ordinary real estate, the online real estate world features real estate agents and property managers. In fact, there are a number of companies that play both roles. Mohit runs one such company: BlackBook investments.

Digital Products

is our education system so perfect and the range of human interests so limited that after finishing their formal education, people are utterly uninterested in supplementing their education? Of course not! And do those people always look for a university or continuing education school, or are they willing to consider online options? Of course they are! And we're not just talking about online degrees. We're talking about digital education products designed to teach you what you need to know to solve a particular problem or improve at something. From your poker game to building an online business to improving your health, there are an endless array of best-selling digital education products.

The online learning industry, as it is often called, earned $107 Billion in 2015, according to a Forbes estimate.[7] Bigger and bigger companies are getting into the act, as LinkedIn's purchase of Lynda.com would suggest (prior to

---

[7] http://www.forbes.com/sites/tjmccue/2014/08/27/online-learning-industry-poised-for-107-billion-in-2015/#33b059e166bc

Microsoft buying LinkedIn!) There are two simple ways you can get into the business: You can promote someone else's products in exchange for commissions or you can create your own products. As you might expect, the first option is lower-risk and is less capital-intensive but has lower ultimate rewards and the second option is higher-risk/more capital-intensive but has higher ultimate rewards.

If you take the lower-risk option, please refer to the previous chapter on niche websites – as niche websites are a great vehicle for promoting other people's products. If you're interested in the second option, read on.

This is an income stream that will be far easier to get started with if you've done much of the self-awareness work that we recommended in the first chapter. That's because you will need to search within yourself to identify expertise for the mass-market or at least, expertise that is attractive to an easily identifiable niche market.

If you're looking to reach the mass-market, there are three tried-and-true subject areas that are a great place to start:

1. Helping people get paid
2. Helping people get laid
3. Helping people lose weight

It doesn't get much more fundamental in terms of human needs than those! Obviously, all three are massive offline industries because they help people solve their most pressing problems. There are now plenty of online businesses – some with good products and some with not so good products – teaching people how to solve those problems. That there is plenty of competition in the digital products world is not a reason to be intimidated– it's a sign that there are buyers. Platforms like Facebook and Instagram offer access to hundreds of millions of potential buyers so there's plenty of room for more market entrants.

And the best part – as with online real estate, is that even if you know nothing about the internet, you can hire others to do much of the work for you. After you've chosen a subject area and a market, it's about deciding which strategy you wish to implement:

1. Do it entirely by yourself

2. Hire a coach to help you figure out what to do and hold you accountable
3. Hire someone or a larger team to do everything for you (other than the content production)

Our section on passive vs. active income streams will be extremely helpful in understanding which strategy makes the most sense for you. Take stock of how much time and money you're willing to invest. Be honest with yourself. Do you tend to finish what you start or do you initially tend to get excited about new projects and then lose interest? If you fit into the second category, acknowledge that – don't pretend otherwise. If you don't have the money to turn this into more of a passive income stream, and you don't have the work ethic to take path #1, don't do this. Do something else.

Even if you opt for option #3, this is a slightly less passive income stream than hiring someone to run a niche website for you, as in that case you don't have to play any role at all in content creation. Here, the business will be branded in your name and you must produce the content. It has to be in your genuine voice and represent the culmination of your years of experience. It has to be an area where you really have a lot to contribute.

If you opt for option 1, here are the basic steps you'll need to implement:

1. Build a list of products of increasing value and cost. The sales funnels for many digital products consists of 5-7 products/services with a price list along these lines: $27, $47, $97, $500, $3000.
2. Build the products – you can create PowerPoint/Screenshare videos and you can provide the voiceovers.
3. Grab a website with an FTP so you can upload the products.
4. Build an email list using a service like AWeber or GetResponse
5. Create some free content – sometimes referred to as "free lead bait".

6. Build a squeeze page so you can collect people's email addresses.
7. Create a sales page for each product.
8. Drive traffic to the free content using either paid ads like Facebook ads (costs more money than time) or write free content and advertise it on social media (costs more time than money) or both.
9. Test every element of your funnel. Start with your ads if you're running ads – what kind of metrics are you getting? If the ads are cost-effective and driving people to your free lead bait, are people opting in to your email list? If not, test a different free lead bait. Etc.

As you can see, this process is not for the faint of heart. But the hard work will pay off if you're willing to invest the time and money as this is a phenomenal business model – a products business with the potential for extraordinary passive income, a marketing machine that can reach around the world in a cost-effective manner and no inventory costs or product purchasing costs – remember, the products are all digital.

Another great option, if you don't want the hassle of going through all of the above but still want to spread your teachings via the Internet would be to use platforms like Udemy and Teachable.

If you're interested in option 2, here are some good providers to explore, both in the $3,000 range:

1. Ramit Sethi's *Zero to Launch* course. His course will help you come up with the subject matter and show you the steps you need to test your market before you launch and make sure that your products are solving people's problems. He also has a large team behind him that will help to hold you accountable. They will call you and be sure that you are doing the work you committed to do. His course is not always open but you can sign up for his email list, which will tell you when it is going to open up, here:

2. James Francis' *Zero to 10k Coaching*. He is laser-focused on helping you build a digital products business. He runs a $60,000 per month digital products business himself. The program consists of very specific videos and you can ask James questions. He responds on a daily basis.

If you're interested in option 3, you should check out James' Francis *Ultimate Done For You Service* where for $10,000 he will do all of the work for you except creating the content. And it comes with a guarantee that you get a full refund if he does not create a $10,000 per month business for you, by the 12-month mark. Take it from us: James is the real deal. It isn't every day that you get offered a $10,000 per month business on a silver platter!

Prediction Markets

You may hear that when it comes to starting a business, your interests and hobbies are not especially useful. But the things you obsess about when you're not working can be the source of a great new income stream. Prediction markets are a great mechanism for you to monetize interests that have nothing to do with business such as: sports, the Oscars, politics, etc. Have you heard of prediction markets?

The Wikipedia definition says prediction markets are: "exchange-traded markets created for the purpose of trading the outcome of events. The market prices can indicate what the crowd thinks the probability of the event is. A prediction market contract trades between 0 and 100%. It is a binary option that will expire at the price of 0 or 100%."

The CIA, academics, pollsters and policymakers use prediction markets. We are all struggling with an uncertain world but some of us know more than others about particular aspects of the uncertainty. That's where the money is. On most prediction markets, the odds of an event occurring are reflected in the price; where the market believes there is a 78% chance of an event occurring, you can purchase shares for $7.80 and those shares can rocket to $10 or $0 if the event occurs or does not occur, respectively. Some prediction markets also allow you to create short positions.

We will give you an example to be sure you understand. In early 2012, Dan became convinced that Barack Obama would win re-election. The then most popular prediction market, Intrade, rated Obama's chances of re-election at 54%. Dan and some of his friends agreed with famed electoral Nostradamus, Nate Silver, that Obama's chances were far higher than that. Obsessed with presidential politics, Dan was confident of his prediction and was able to convince others to invest in a small fund that would in turn purchase Obama shares on Intrade. If Obama was victorious, the price would increase to $10 per share and fall to $0, if Obama lost. Make no mistake - this was risky business. Luckily, there were plenty of ways to hedge. At any rate, the potential for gains was great. In Canada, prediction market income is considered gambling income by tax authorities, so all gains are tax-free as of October 2016. This meant that had we lost, our losses would not have been tax-deductible. You should, of course, not assume this is the case in other countries or that the law cannot change in Canada.

Unfortunately, Intrade is no longer. But there is another operational real money prediction market: PredictIt. They have limits, so you can't make hundreds of thousands as you could on Intrade. But this space is changing constantly so you can create Google Alerts to watch for new prediction markets. Take a look at PredictIt's list of markets and see if any of them relate to your areas of knowledge.

University Tutoring

Higher education is big business but universities and colleges are not the only ones who can profit. Subpar teaching – particularly professors' inability to reach students without a natural gift for the material or those with learning disabilities, means many students need tutors. Standardized tests like the GMAT, GRE, LSAT and MCAT are also great opportunities for aspiring tutors. If you've got a university degree, or even if you're doing one right now, you could be well-positioned to build a tutoring income stream. If you can teach math, accounting, finance, the hard sciences, the GMAT or economics, you may have more demand than you can handle.

If I ask you what you think the default price for a tutor would be, what would you say? Take a moment and think. We're willing to bet that many of you would say something like $20, $25 or $30 an hour. Many tutors charge those paltry amounts. But with some negotiating tips under your belt, you should be able to charge considerably more. And there are plenty of platforms that do much of the marketing for you so that you can just focus on providing the best possible educational experience for clients.

Start by creating an account on one of the tutoring platforms. Dan uses University Tutor. If you're able to tutor multiple subjects, you'll want to start by determining which tutors in your area are making the most money. A good proxy for this on University Tutor is the number of five-star reviews they've obtained. Other platforms also have a five-star rating system. You can also draw inspiration from the way in which they've written their profiles. Tutor a friend or two to start, for free if necessary, so you can obtain one or two initial five-star reviews.

We recommend not indicating a price on your profile. This will lead users to ask you what your price is. It is tempting to respond with a number. Dan has achieved great results by asking leads what their tutoring budget is. Often, leads will respond by asking you what your typical rate is. Again, we recommend resisting the urge to respond with a number.

This is because people have wildly different expectations about what tutoring should cost. Where this is the case, it's ideal to determine each individual prospect's price expectations. Where a prospect expects you to tutor them for $20, you probably can't move them up to a price where it is worth your while – unless you are truly desperate for cash. But you at least have a chance to do so, whereas if you named a price of, say, $60, they would run for the hills.

On the flip side, you may name a price that is too low and you would never have known that a client was willing to pay more than your asking price. You'd be amazed at how much some people are willing to pay for good tutoring. If you are confident in what you do and have any kind of credential in the field, you can cite that credential as a reason why you charge more than normal. You can make your tutoring risk-free by offering a money-back guarantee if the client is dissatisfied.

Dan has charged up to $200/hr for tutoring and university admissions consulting. There are admissions consulting companies in the US, particularly for MBA applicants, that charge far more than that. The big lesson is to not trust your initial assumptions about what the market will bear. You must test the market and see how it responds. If you don't, you may be leaving plenty of money on the table.

Real Estate

Real estate is an excellent solution for an investor who wants to build generational wealth and accumulate enough money to offset inflation while preventing erosion of their savings by taxes. You can invest in real estate passively or actively. Active real estate entrepreneurs purchase properties after which they repair and/or improve them and eventually sell them for profit. Passive real estate investors hire real estate companies to find investment properties and manage them on their behalf.

A major reason why people choose real estate entrepreneurship is because they believe real estate fares better than other investments like stocks, even when the economy is bad. After all, land is a finite resource and people will always need a place to not just live and work, but also to play. Thus, real estate continues to appreciate even with occasional economic downs. Today, real estate investments like rental properties, commercial properties, self-storage facilities, mobile parks and apartment complexes are major income streams for many investors.

Now you might be thinking that investing in real estate requires a lot of capital. Well, I would beg to differ. Today, you don't necessarily have to be a real estate investor to reap its benefits; you can be a real estate entrepreneur. A real estate entrepreneur is someone who benefits from the money-making opportunities that real estate provides, regardless of whether they have money to invest or not.

Here are some ways in which you can make money and create wealth using real estate.

1. Flipping houses

Flipping houses means purchasing properties at discounted prices and selling them at higher prices. Usually, you must improve the property between 30 and 60 days to increase its value and make a profit from its sale. To make money from house flipping, you must choose houses in areas where the prices of residential properties are rising. However, this can be a risky approach, especially when prices rise due to an asset bubble after which they fall once the bubble bursts.

2. Rental properties

Real estate investors purchase rental properties that they rent out to others. This has long been the traditional method of real estate investing and it still works like a charm. This approach includes considerable expenses like maintenance, upkeep, closing costs, property tasks, problematic tenants and possible existing debts. It is a sensible approach when there is a net positive after deducting expenses from rental income. Remember, you want to invest in cash-flow positive properties.

3. Real estate securities

You can also invest in the real estate securities that include municipal bonds and REITs. REITs or Real Estate Investment Trusts are securitized limited partnerships and they trade in the capital markets on the basis of the value of the limited partnership. Municipal bonds, on the other hand, are issued by states and cities to raise money for various municipal initiatives like construction projects. Investing in securities is basically investing in the public properties.

4. P2P Lending

This entails investing in loans with real estate as collateral, also known as First Trust Deed Investing. With this approach, you become the private source of money and loan a borrower, who is typically a real estate expert or company. The borrower invests the money for long-term holds in the real estate. A Trust Deed is the document that secures the investment in the real estate loan.

5. Commercial properties

Some real estate entrepreneurs specialize in investing in commercial properties. This entails developing portfolios of their properties. This investment approach provides a lucrative rental income while the properties appreciate in value over the years. In most cases, these real estate entrepreneurs roll over their profits into new properties, usually a 1031 exchange while leaving management firms to run their properties.

Some entrepreneurs make fortunes by purchasing, improving and selling commercial properties. This is similar to house flipping but some entrepreneurs hold on to properties as they wait for their prices to appreciate while they earn rental income from them. Such properties include office spaces, retail storefronts, hotels, apartment complexes and entertainment venues like concert halls and casinos.

6. Mortgage notes

Another ingenious way to make money from real estate is by buying and selling mortgage notes from and to other investors, financial entities and banks. As a mortgage note owner, you own the mortgage debt of the homeowner. Therefore, you are entitled to mortgage payments that the homeowner may otherwise pay to the mortgage originator such as the bank.

7. Wholesaling

Most real estate entrepreneurs with limited capital start by wholesaling properties because it teaches them the basics of real estate entrepreneurship. Wholesaling entails getting a property under a contract and selling it or assigning the contract quickly to someone else for a small profit.

You can wholesale that property to a different investor who flips it. To get a successful property wholesale deal, you must find a cheap property that gives you room for making profit when you sell it. Ideally, the rule of thumb is to get a property under contract for 70% (or less) of its market value.

Each of these strategies for making money from real estate entrepreneurship entails conducting market research, setting financial goals, finding the right asset, financing it and receiving income from its sale or renting it out to earn rental income. Ideally, successful real estate entrepreneurs take time to estimate the return on investment of properties that they purchase. This enables them to evaluate their worth and possible profits that can be earned from their future sale.

Perhaps, you think that real estate entrepreneurship is reserved for those with high amounts of capital. The truth is that you don't need a lot of money to start making money from real estate using some of the above approaches. In fact, you can start with wholesaling properties which does not require a lot of money and can quickly help you generate capital. Once you have capital, you can invest in the right properties in any of the above ways that suit you. Here are some pointers to do real estate the smart way.

1. Capitalize on physical assets

Income-producing properties are among the classes of hard asset investments that have meaningful value. The land on which a property is built and the structure itself have value. The income that the structure produces also yields value for the investor. With a physical asset, you will never have green and red days because you will earn income every month from your real estate when you invest in physical assets.

2. Hedge on the inflation

For each created dollar, there is a liability that corresponds to it. Historically, investments in real estate have shown greater correlation with inflation than other investments. Whenever there is inflation, real estate prices, especially multi-tenant properties with high labor to replacement ratios, increase.

3. Multiply your asset value using leverage

With commercial real estate, you can place debt on your asset. This is usually several times your original equity. Doing so enables you to purchase more assets with limited finances and multiply your asset value significantly while increasing equity as your loans are repaid.

4. Plan financial goals

It is important that you determine what exactly you want to achieve from real estate entrepreneurship by setting financial goals. Consider the "time versus money" concept before you make any real estate investment by taking your time to ensure that the investment that you make leads you to achieving your financial goals. However, though you need to learn the basics of real estate entrepreneurship, don't spend more resources on books, seminars and tapes than you do on the actual investments.

Take time to consider the available properties and ensure that you don't purchase a property just because it looks nice. Avoid falling into the analysis paralysis trap but conduct thorough research on properties and ways of making money from real estate investment. Nevertheless, real estate remains popular due to the ever-rising values of properties.

P2P Lending

P2P lending is also called social lending, marketplace lending or platform lending. It refers to a system that allows institutional and individual investors to fund direct loans to individual borrowers for education, credit card consolidation, vacation and home improvement purposes. Companies like Prosper and Lending Club act as the intermediaries between lenders and borrowers. These are responsible for handling delinquent loans, fee assessments, fund transfers, record keeping, and other tasks.

Investors earn monthly interest and principal payments as passive income when borrowers repay loans. The entire process is not passive because as an investor, you have to conduct research when selecting your initial investment or when you want to reinvest proceeds or even set up an automatic investing system on the basis of your preferences.

As an investor, you choose the company that you want to use as your peer to peer lending platform. Ideally, you will not be charged any fee because most P2P lenders charge borrowers a fee. However, you may be charged by the intermediary company after a borrower pays the loan. Here is how the P2P lending process works:

1. The interested borrower fills out a loan application form.
2. Experts from the intermediary company evaluate the application and set an interest rate for the loan.
3. Different loan offers are presented to the borrower.
4. The borrower picks their preferred loan option after which it is activated on the website.
5. An investor chooses a loan for their portfolio and selects the amount of the loan they would like to fund. As an investor, you can fund as little as $25, a fraction known as the Note.
6. Once an investor or investors fund the loan fully, the intermediary company transfers the fund into the bank account of the borrower directly.

7. The borrower pays the loan each month and the intermediary company deposits returns and interests into the account of the investor.
8. As an investor, you can withdraw your money or reinvest it.

Peer to peer lending is an investment that makes both financial sense and human sense since it enables you to make money while helping another person who is in need of that money. It gives you a monthly flow of cash with low volatility, compared to other investments like the stock market. Additionally, despite the fact that this is not a scheme for making quick profit, it allows you to either withdraw or reinvest your cash.

The lending process for an ideal P2P intermediary allows for a broad diversification, even for small investors. This means that you do not have to invest all your funds in one loan. You can allocate the funds in small amounts of $25 to different loans. Thus, if a borrower defaults, you will be out $25 maximum on a single loan.

This approach makes your P2P lending investment less risky than when you invest $1,000 in a single loan. Based on the default rates and returns of most P2P lending intermediaries like the Lending Club and Prosper, you cannot lose money when you invest $25 in a minimum of 100 loans. Nevertheless, returns are higher on higher-risk paper due to diversification.

Though you might be tempted to start lending money with the hope of earning 3 to 4 times your investment, it is important that you learn a few things.

- P2P investment is about purchasing unsecured loans. According to Lending Club, borrowers have been paying an average rate of 12.6% annually over the last quarter.
- Selling a note is not as easy as selling a bond if you want your money immediately. You can only sell a loan through the investment trading platform of the intermediary company. Typically, a loan is sold within five business days at an average price that is

the same as the outstanding balance. Thus, if for instance you purchased a note at $25 and a borrower has paid down a principal of $10, your outstanding balance portion for the loan will be $15.

- The loan that you buy is as good as your chosen P2P lending company. If something goes wrong with the lending company, you might still be unlucky even when the borrower makes all payments. Economically, transactions with this lending are peer to peer. However, legally, you invest in notes that the lending company issues.

When you start out with peer to peer lending, it is important to have an investment strategy that enables you to leverage your funds for maximum returns. Come up with filters, must-haves or rules before you determine the notes to choose. For instance, your P2P lending investment strategy can be a borrower's checklist for the following:

- A home that a borrower must own

- Employed for the last two years
- Less than three credit report inquiries in the last six months
- Must be looking for a credit card loan
- One year since the last delinquency

Basically, consider what you can check when a friend asks you to lend them money as a way of ensuring that in addition to assisting them, you also reclaim your money with interest.

Interest rates on fixed, safe income investments are generally very low. However, P2P lending provides an opportunity for investors to earn dramatically higher returns from their investments. Ideally, you can earn average returns of 5.06% to 8.74% from your investments with P2P lending. Actually, P2P lending provides alternatives that are outside traditional opportunities for both investors and borrowers.

Nevertheless, the risks of P2P lending are more than those of traditional investments. This explains the attractive rates for P2P lending. Additionally, notes for P2P lending are not available in every country and there may be income requirements that you must meet to invest in P2P lending. If you are looking for a way to earn a little more from your money, P2P lending platforms like Kiva Prosper and Lending Club are ideal for investing some of your savings.

Intellectual Property and Royalties

What do you think of the idea of making money from other people's songs, films, books or technology? Until recently, you probably never had the opportunity to own income-producing intellectual property. This income is what is referred to as royalties.

Royalties are payments to owners for the use of intellectual property, especially copyrighted works, patents, franchises or natural resources. They are paid to the legal owner of the patent, property, copyrighted work or franchises by those who wish to use it to generate revenue or other activities.

They are expressed as a percentage of the revenues obtained using the owner's property, but they are often negotiated to meet the specific needs of any given arrangement. For musicians, inventors, script writers, authors and other owners of intellectual property, royalties are a wonderful way of making money for years without putting in extra effort from re-sales of their products and ideas.

For example, all computer manufacturers pay royalties to Microsoft to be able to use the Windows operating system on the PCs they manufacture;] TV satellite companies provide royalties for airing the most viewed stations; oil and gas companies pay royalties to landowners in order to be allowed to extract natural resources from the covered property.

Some people sell their royalties. There is no doubt that the promise of money every time a record is played or a book is sold is a dream that every creator would want to hold on to. But this is not always the case. For example, a struggling musician may be short of cash when he/she urgently needs to push their career to the next level. If they can't get a bank loan, they will inevitably look for other ways of raising the much needed-cash. This is when selling royalties of their existing creations becomes an immediate source of revenue. For the buyers, owning music royalties could translate to a decent income for life, but only if they invest in the right creations.

What are the different types of royalties to invest in?

There are various types of royalties to invest in. These range from digital rights to performance income. Producers and song writers earn royalties every time their music is performed in public, whether it is via TV, radio, clubs, bars, restaurants, concerts or online streaming services. These royalties are often collected by performing rights organizations before being distributed to producers and songwriters.Mechanical royalties - these are paid to producers, songwriters and recording artists based on the number of recordings sold. These royalties are typically paid via the record company which then distributes the money to various players accordingly.**Performance royalties** – performance royalties are straightforward - a musician earns money when their music is performed publicly through broadcast on radio or TV.**Synchronization royalties** - these are paid to rights owners when their creations are used in connection with visual images such as films, TV adverts, TV programs and video games.

Other royalties - Intellectual property owners earn money via other royalties when, for example, music is streamed as well as ringtones, print music, toys, stage products, and other novelty items.

Making money from purchasing royalties to other peoples' works is fairly easy. For instance, if a producer/artist wants to make some instant cash from their project, they would sell off some of their royalties to buyers. While they would still retain the rights to those tracks, they would be obliged to share part of their income with the buyers whenever the tracks are played on the radio.

To purchase royalties easily, you simply bid for the available ones and if you bid turns out to be the highest, you win. You will then get royalties paid to you, usually quarterly or bi-annually, and for a certain period of time depending on the buying agreement.

The best place to purchase royalties is Royalty Exchange where they charge a 2.5 percent buyer premium and an additional 2.5 percent for the management and payout of your royalty stream.

To maximize revenue from your royalties, follow the steps outlined below:

1. Purchase rights to an in-demand product with a clearly identifiable consumer group.

2. Identify companies whose products could be complemented with the creations you have obtained royalties for. You could perform an internet search using keywords linked to the type of products the creations could sell.

3. Develop relations with decision makers for these companies. Identify the decision makers, and then set up a meeting to pitch your project.

4. Keep track of the company once it adopts your products and starts marketing it or using it for marketing. Sometimes, your partners may ask you to support their marketing efforts. You have to be on hand to keep track of the progress and provide any needed support.

5. Monitor the results

The way you monitor the results depends on how the initial deal was structured. For example, if you paid a royalty based on the sales promotions, downloads or number of times a track is streamed, you will be emailed this information on a regular basis.

Remember, making deals with large companies is the easiest way of making money from royalties you purchased.

Royalties are relatively low risk investments that can keep earning money for you for a very long time without requiring much effort on your part. Most royalty deals are structured to last over 70 years or more, even after the death of the initial rights owners. This is why Michael Jackson's worth increased drastically after his death. According to Billboard, MJ Inc. raked in revenues of no less than $1 billion a year after his death.

On the other hand, though, it is not always possible to make huge sums of cash from royalties and it may take years before you can start enjoying actual returns on the investment. Just like with any other investment, you should analyze the likelihood of that particular film, song, book, product being in demand for many years. If you are lucky to invest in a long-term winner, you can be assured of a reasonable revenue stream for a long time. Avoid buying royalties for products whose popularity has already started waning. The good thing is that you can purchase royalties for a variety of products and set up as many deals as you wish.

Freelancing

Are you tired of the routine and monotony associated with your regular 9-5 day job? Would you like to free yourself of the shackles and nerve-wracking commitments of regular employment? Are you interested in a flexible way of generating constant income from the comfort and convenience of your own home? Then you should consider freelancing as a viable option for generating income.

As the name implies, there is an element of freedom. Try to think of freelancing as a form of self-employment. As a freelancer, you pick the jobs you want and do them at your own convenience, of course within reason. So long as you possess the right skills, you can pick whatever job you like and do it to the best of your abilities.

The following are a few tips and pointers that should get you started if you want to go the freelance way:

1. **Have a clear vision of what you can do**

You need to identify your skills first and decide what kind of projects you can take on. To be honest, you do not need a lot of experience to get started with freelance jobs.

Just believe in yourself and your abilities and get started. One of the greatest obstacles to freelance work is a negative attitude and the feeling that you cannot do it.

2. **Develop and build your portfolio.**

Your demonstration of and ability to get the job done are more important to clients than your experience and qualifications. In this regard, ensure that you have a portfolio that has samples of your previous work and projects for your clients. Reviews and testimonials from your past clients and companies that you have worked for will be a welcome addition to your portfolio and add strength and credibility to it.

3. **Create and market your brand**

Get out there and start pitching yourself to potential clients. Once you cast a wide net, you are bound to get a few freelance jobs to get you started. Be persistent and relentless in your pursuit of freelance jobs and remember, follow up is the key.

4. Be business savvy in your approach

You need to be conversant with the basics of running a business as a freelancer. You need to know the basics of bookkeeping, filing tax returns, sales, and marketing in order to succeed. One thing you should take care of is the self-employment tax, if it applies to you.

5. Setup your payment and invoicing system

As a freelancer, you need to realize that you are no longer on a payroll. You need to manage your finances. Set up a system of invoicing and receiving payments. This will enable you to be organized and keep track of how much money and profits you are raking in from your freelance jobs. You can use tools like FreshBooks and Stripe to help you in bookkeeping and invoicing.

6. **Have patience**

With freelancing, exercise a lot of prudence and avoid throwing caution to the wind. You will be able to earn decent money as a freelancer but it takes some time to build up.

7. **Prepare for dry spells**

You need to brace yourself for those periods when there will be little or no freelance work for you to do. However, be encouraged, as these dry spells do not last for long if you've taken lesson 3 to heart.

8. **Hold yourself accountable**

As a freelancer, you are entirely responsible for your work and actions. Be prepared to bear the consequences of your own laxity.

There are many online freelancing sites where you can get work. You will find work broadly classified into writing, sales and marketing, tutoring and consultancy, graphic design, website and software development, social media and SEO (search engine optimization). That being said, freelancing is not limited to these categories. Some of the most common freelancing sites that you can consider include the following:

1. **Upwork**

Upwork is arguably one of the best sites to find freelance jobs. Whether you are a designer, attorney, financial designer or IT professional, there is plenty of freelance work available for you. Start out by setting up your profile on Upwork. For individual projects, you can either have a fixed price or charge an hourly rate. Depending on how well you do the job, you will be rated accordingly, which would determine your ability to get future jobs.

2. **Freelancer**

Since its inception in 2004, Freelancer has had a large following of freelancers. If you are interested in data entry, marketing or writing jobs, which happen to be a specialty of this platform, you can easily get work from Freelancer.

3. **Guru**

Guru.com is a large network of over 1.5 million freelancers and is one of the oldest freelancing platforms. The website specifically state that they are interested in working on "technical, creative or business projects". If you are a video game developer, programmer, engineer, or translator, Guru.com can offer you lots of opportunities.

4. **People Per Hour**

People Per Hour is a UK based company that has gained popularity in recent times. Like Upwork, it offers you a lot of categories to work in. You can even create interesting short videos that promote you and your services.

5. **Fiverr**

Fiverr is a unique platform where you can start selling your services for $5. You can create unique DIY projects, write and perform interesting poems or even create one of a kind promotional videos. Some of the best freelance job categories on Fiverr include video animations, programming, writing and translation, online marketing, music and graphic design.

6. **99Designs**

99Designs.com has over 280,000 designers who come from almost 200 countries worldwide. If you are a designer, this platform allows you to connect with potential clients and highlight your works of art. Potential clients will give an outline of the work they expect or the type of logo they want. You and many other designers then work on the client's request. The client then picks which piece of work suits them best.

7. Art Wanted

If you are a great artist or photographer, then Art Wanted is where you want to be. All you need to do is to create your online portfolio and get feedback from the site. Once you are in the clear, you can start selling your artwork online.

8. Pitch Me

Are you a journalist looking for freelance work? Pitchme.org offers you a chance to pitch your journalistic ideas to potential clients on topics ranging from fashion to culture.

How much can you earn?

This is heavily dependent on the nature of your work and how much demand there is for it. Programmers tend to do better than designers and writers. If you've got an MBA from a good school, you can earn hundreds of dollars per hour on MBA & Company, Skillbridge, and other sites focused on MBAs. Fiverr and Upwork allow you to see how much freelancers charge per hour.

If you seem to be getting bored with your regular day job and want freedom and relief from your boss breathing down your neck, try freelancing. As a freelancer, you get to set your own rules and flexible work schedule. However, freelancing requires self-discipline, determination, patience and hard work on your part. Nothing comes easy.

Coaching

To earn money from coaching, a combination of professional experience, business-related skills and personal qualities are required. As a coach, you can work for small and large companies, government organizations, entrepreneurs, universities and non-profit organizations.

Your role as a coach is to assist businesses and individuals to identify long-term objectives, improve business processes, resolve interpersonal conflicts and create skills development plans. Here are some practical strategies for making money as a coach:

Create a niche for yourself

In order to make more money as a coach, you need to answer the question, "what can I personally offer my clients in terms of my areas of expertise apart from the professional training as a coach?" As soon as you identify your main area of training such as personal, business or career coaching, you can then single out and concentrate on a particular niche so as to build niche expertise and reputation which clients covet.

One-on-one coaching clients

One-on-one coaching, in my opinion, is one of the most effective ways to make money from coaching. Most coaches usually spend approximately 1-2 hours every week with each client. The most effective way to make sure you'll have the chance to engage a profitable client is to identify businesses with at least 25 employees. This group can afford coaching and is much more comfortable with spending on coaching. After about two months of working with senior officers of the organization, you can start to offer your services to the leadership team and include the employees, too.

Study other top earners

Identify some of the most successful coaches who are recognizable and charge the highest fees for the services they provide. Look at what their clients say about them, how they manage to grow the businesses they work with, and also how they market themselves.

Rather than hours or monthly fees, offer packages

The worst mistake that you should avoid at all costs is to offer your coaching services by the hour or on a monthly basis. This will not only hurt your clients but also compromise your earnings. It will hurt your clients because they will not be enrolled with the long-term mindset, but rather a quick fix. Results don't come overnight, they take time; and the clients who are in a six month or one year engagement get the most value. In addition, the higher your coaching fee, the more clients will value your services.

Increase your fees

One of the simplest ways to earn more money from your coaching career is to increase your prices. But before you do this, observe these two things. First, you need to have a better reputation than that of your competitors to justify your prices. What makes you more valuable than all other coaches? Secondly, you must prove to your clients that the benefit to their businesses will be much higher than the fees you are charging. You may show them how much money past clients have saved or their increased revenues to prove your worth.

Increase your demand

Most coaches don't charge as much as they should because they do not market themselves, hence they become desperate for clients. When you're in demand for your services, it's a hundred times easier to charge your value. The best way to set yourself up for success is by having a marketing system that offers plenty of leads for your coaching business.

Negotiate success fees

You may also up your fees by adding a provision for success fees in the contract. This fee is charged when your client's business reaches a given performance milestone during the time you are working with them or after. This will motivate you to work even harder so as to attain your set goals. It also reassures your clients that their money will be safe should you fail to deliver.

Ask for testimonials

Written or video testimonials from your satisfied clients are a very powerful tool for credibility in the market, and also very good for your coaching business. When you are going through those challenging days and you want to be reminded that you are a wonderful coach, listen to what your past clients have said about you.

Share in your clients' success

Making your pay dependent on the success of your client's is another potential way to increase your earnings. For instance, you can set your fees as a percentage of the revenue increase realized by your client as a result of your services. Make sure that when you do this, it's on contract. The earning potential from this arrangement can be quite huge.

Always invest in your business

A majority of coaches live a hundred percent off their coaching earnings, and invest almost nothing back in developing their business. If you save money for your business, you will be able to hire people like a social media manager to market yourself better and also advertise in your target market's preferred magazines, newspapers, websites etc. The more you are able to invest in your business, the faster it is likely to grow, and the more your earnings will increase.

Holding group coaching programs

Group coaching is also another valuable service you can offer. It's an outstanding way to leverage your time and, at the same time, help as many clients as possible. It is the most effective way to include clients who cannot afford one-on-one coaching fees. You may charge around $500 to $1000 per client per month. Typically, group coaching can be delivered to between four to ten clients at a time. This works best if you have a curriculum that the attendees can follow and learn from.

It is important to have a manual that includes chapters and homework assignments clients can use to follow along every week. Ideally, every group coaching session should last for 1-2 hours, and then a twenty-minute question answer session.

If you are interested in starting a career as a coach, Clarity.fm and Presto Experts can be good places to start. Coach.me is a great platform for acquiring new clients though you'll have to revenue share if they send you clients.

Sharing Economy (AirBnB, Uber)

Are you generous to a fault and love sharing your stuff with other people? Are you comfortable lending your colleague at work your guest room to accommodate his visiting cousin? Would you lend your buddy your pickup truck for the weekend without even thinking twice? Would you like to make some extra cash from your generosity? Then you need to start considering the sharing economy and how you can make money from it.

The sharing economy is a broad term that encompasses various social and economic activities that usually involve online transactions. The term, sharing economy, is currently used to describe any sales transactions like business to consumer transactions that are done on online marketplaces.

In simpler terms, the sharing economy refers to an economic model where individuals rent or borrow assets that belong to other individuals. This model is mostly used when a particular asset's price is high, yet that asset is not fully used all the time. Ideally, the sharing economy enables groups and individuals to make money from the underused assets. Thus, they share physical assets as services. Peer to peer accommodation, social lending, car sharing, travel advising and peer to peer travel experiences are some of the emerging sectors that make use of the sharing economy.

A good example of a sharing economy model is when a car owner allows another person to rent out their vehicle when they are not using it. You could even buy a car solely to use it on car sharing services like Getaround. Another example is when a condo owner rents out their condo while on vacation. As the cloud and mobile computing services become increasingly prevalent, the scope and scale of this economic model is growing rapidly.

Examples of platforms for making money from the sharing economy

The sharing economy has numerous pieces. For instance, peer to peer marketplaces bring individual sellers and buyers together in a direct manner. This is a two-sided marketplace that is maintained by third parties that charge a fee in order to facilitate transactions between sellers and buyers. They also reduce transactional risk. Other platforms or examples of these marketplaces include Airbnb, Uber and Homeaway among others. Platforms like Krrb, Craiglist, Lyft, and Etsy are other examples that allow direct interactions between sellers and buyers.

Other sharing economy sectors include the open-source software that allows the interested parties to view and alter computer codes for different software projects without incurring extra costs. Napste,r for instance, marked the beginning of a file sharing system that has evolved into different legit ways of sharing content legally via platforms like Netflix and Spotify.

Crowdfunding platforms give inventors and entrepreneurs the ability to get funds without relying on traditional financing institutions like banks. Bitcoin is an example of decentralized digital currencies that provide a viable means of ensuring reliable transactions without involving a central bank or traditional money.

How to Benefit from the Sharing Economy

Creation of new services

The demand for services like short-term apartment rentals and ride sharing that traditional means cannot easily meet due to the required capital investment, is growing. Uber has successfully used this economic model due to its service ubiquity. The transportation firm requires a massive fleet of cars and drivers. This can be very expensive if the company opted to supply the cars and hire all the drivers for full-time jobs. Thus, if the company did not employ the sharing economy, it could not provide its services. According to Uber, drivers make an average of $19 per hour. There was even news of an Uber driver (or Uberpreneur, if you will) who made $250,000 in one year, driving Uber. He did this by selling other goods and services to passengers.

Mutual growth

The sharing economy enables small businesses and companies to benefit from co-working spaces and shared offices. These have popped up in different parts of the world. Transforming a small business into a properly shared office is easier than you might think. For instance, you can start by renting out an entire room to another company. You can also rent out one desk and bring in money while giving your businesses an opportunity to connect. This can bolster mutual growth for the businesses that share the space.

Outsourcing

Your small business might not have a huge team. However, this should not limit its growth. When you need an important task to be carried out, hiring an expert on a full-time basis is not always a practical solution. This is where you turn to outsourcing and the sharing economy. Today, there are numerous platforms via which you can hire an individual to perform almost any task.

The sharing economy can benefit you even offline. For instance, as a small travel business owner in Rome, you may want to learn the Roman culture for a crucial business meeting. In that case, you can hire a local person to teach you. That person will teach you almost everything, including cultural aspects like how people greet each other during the first meeting, how to eat and how to use hand gestures while speaking. This is a cost-effective way of running that particular aspect of your business because you only pay for that specific task.

Generally, the sharing economy creates stronger communities where people share assets that they are not using thereby saving costs for some people and allowing others access to goods that they cannot afford. It increases flexibility, independence, and self-reliance while accelerating sustainable production and consumption patterns in different places across the world. Thus, apart from benefiting individuals and businesses, the sharing economy has also changed how businesses operate.

Five ways you can make money from the sharing economy

1. Rent out your spare room

Airbnb is a great example of how you can make money through the sharing economy. Airbnb can help you to get accommodation in over 30,000 cities located in 192 countries all over the world. However, these rooms are not the usual hotel accommodation that you are used to. AirBnB accommodation options range from a well decked out Airstream or a room in somebody's home. Would you believe that at least 4 million people have used the Airbnb site since its launch in 2008?

You must be wondering how you can make money using AirBnB? If you have a room or two to spare in your home, AirBnB will connect you with travelers or people looking for temporary accommodation. Depending on the location and type of room you list on Airbnb, you can make up to $100 per night or more.

2. Offer somebody a ride

Have you ever thought of making money by offering someone a ride in your car? Well, now you can do that and make money at the same time. All you need to do is to sign up on a ridesharing platform like Uber or Lyft. Once you sign up, you will be able to receive alerts from people who are interested in getting a ride.

Making money on Uber is as simple as picking up your interested clients, dropping them off, getting paid and moving on to your next job. Really, it is that easy.

3. Share your unused stuff

Do you remember that electric drill or aluminum cutter you bought for a specific reason? Do you even remember where you last stored it? You can make money from sharing tools and other stuff you bought and have never had the chance to use again. ShareHammer.com connects you with people in your neighborhood who may want to borrow a particular tool for a few hours or days. All you need to do is to sign up on the site and list the tools that you have on offer for sharing.

4. Lend your extra money

Got some extra cash lying around? You can lend this cash and make some extra money by charging a small interest on the loan. There are peer to peer lending platforms like LendingClub, and Kiva that you can check out. According to LendingClub, as an investor, you can expect returns of about 5% on your safest investment option. You can even get higher returns if you are willing to up the ante in terms of risk. However, when you decide to loan out cash, bear in mind that this comes with the risk of you losing your capital. Just make sure you do not dip into your kid's college fund or your retirement savings.

5. How About Sharing Your Skills and Talent?

Platforms like TaskRabbit and FancyHands let you share your talents and skillset with other people. On TaskRabbit.com, you will find people posting needs like the need for someone to do their housecleaning or shopping.

6. Rent out your parking or driveway

In most major cities around the world, you will find that parking spaces are available at a premium. Services like JustPark.com allow you to share parking space at your place with someone else for a fee. If you live next to a busy airport, you are lucky. You can make over $200 just renting out your parking space to visitors through the airport.

Crowdfunding

Do you happen to belong to a group of like-minded, ambitious individuals who are interested in making investments? Would you be interested in a model that allows you to invest in a business and get to own part of the business you invest in? Are you a novice entrepreneur looking for an investor to pump funds into your business? Then crowdfunding is what you should seek.

Equity crowdfunding entails a group of people investing in a company at its initial stages in exchange for shares in the company. If the company profits and grows, then the investors get a good return on what they put in the company as capital. However, if the company makes losses, then the investors lose their investment in the business. Equity crowdfunding may also be referred to as investment crowdfunding, crowd equity or crowd investing.

Equity crowdfunding has numerous advantages for you as an entrepreneur or investor. Here are some of them:

1. Readily Available Investment Opportunities

Venture capitalists and angel investing markets are clustered together as private investing. Private investing used to be considered opaque, segmented and limited in their investment choices. Well, not anymore. As an investor, you now have access to a much larger investor base thanks to equity crowdfunding.

However, you'll need to factor in the degree of risk that is associated with equity crowdfunding. When you compare equity crowdfunding with other forms of investing like stocks or real estate, it generally has a higher level of risk. If you look at it from a more optimistic viewpoint, equity crowdfunding is a great opportunity for you to enjoy superior returns on your investments. If you've heard of high-risk high-gain ventures, equity crowdfunding certainly falls under this bracket.

2. Legal Advantages

The process of raising funds can be long and tedious. During this lengthy, time-consuming process, new businesses have to pay astronomical legal fees. Since equity crowdfunding is mostly done online, you will find that it takes a much shorter time and your legal costs will be lower.

3. Investor Ease of Access to Startups

If you are an investor, you can benefit greatly from the streamlined crowdfunding process. You can sift through the many listings and identify the ones you want to invest in and that match your investment interests.

4. Investor Vetting

As an entrepreneur, equity crowdfunding allows you to vet any investors who are interested in investing in your business. The investor vetting mechanism allows you to be in control of your fundraising since you make the final choice of whether to deny or approve their investment.

As an investor or entrepreneur with a startup business model, you can see that equity crowdfunding has numerous advantages. If you are an entrepreneur, you will have access to a large pool of investors who might want to invest in your business. You will be able to get guidance from established venture capitalists and investors who will assist you as you start out. As an investor, you will find that online equity crowdfunding enables you to conduct seamless transactions and easily check out companies you want to invest in. Beyond crowdfunding, let's discuss another way you can raise capital.

Raising Capital

Banks are not every borrower's cup of tea. They are very traditional – and conservative. They tend not to be open to taking a risk on a new idea, like many of the income stream concepts we've discussed in this book. Good luck getting a bank to loan you money to acquire a revenue-generating website. Luckily, there's an alternative: A new breed of lender that is far more flexible than a traditional bank.

In the Peer to Peer Lending section, we discussed Lending Club. That's a good example. Ondeck in the US, Canada and Australia and Borrowell in Canada share Lending Club's willingness to lend to a broader array of people and businesses than traditional banks. If you're in the US, we highly recommend you speak to the folks at All Green USA.

The folks at All Green are ex-financial services people who will represent you in negotiations with banks and can get you super low interest rates, especially if you do a secured loan. They can also get you a loan on the basis of your accounts receivable or credit rating.

Productivity

The most valuable trait of a successful business is having a productive entrepreneur at the helm. Making sure that you are properly utilizing every moment throughout the day is the only way to guarantee that you have a streamlined and effective business. But in an age where distractions are as abundant as the water in the ocean, how does one find his or her path to productivity?

We are going to discuss a myriad of ways to increase your productivity. These range from concentration techniques to phone and Internet applications. We are looking to make sure that you have the most cutting-edge ideas at your disposal.

Virtual Assistant/Personal Assistant

You're an entrepreneur. You have multiple accounts and businesses to manage and you don't always have time for every small task throughout the day. Maybe you need to edit a few sales spreadsheets but you are on the way to a meeting and don't have time. This would be the perfect situation to have a personal assistant to take care of some of the day's most basic and repetitive tasks.

These assistants, depending on whether you choose a virtual or personal one, can perform simple tasks from fetching you lunch to scheduling your appointments to taking phone calls. Venture Capitalists and successful businessmen such as Mark Suster and Tony Robbins strongly advocate the implementation of a personal assistant into your entrepreneur lifestyle. There are numerous reputable virtual and personal assistant services on the web where you can get started. Zirtual and Fancy Hands are two such examples.

Blocking Distractions and Keeping Momentum

As we mentioned earlier, we live in an age of distractions. Facebook notifications, email notification, text messages, calendars and a whirlwind of other obligations that can get in the way of your daily progress. How do we find a way to bottleneck some of these notifications and sift through some of the white noise that keeps us from achieving productivity? Apps like

Focus and FocusMe help you accomplish tasks by blocking out distracting websites and helping you focus on the task at hand.

You can also use the Pomodoro Technique to crush tasks and build momentum. This technique might sound like some martial art taught by a Tibetan Monk but it is actually a popular time-saving technique used by some of the most successful business people in the world. This technique is based on working in short intense intervals and then taking short breaks in between as a mental refresher. A good way to implement this technique is by using a timer and setting two different alarms, one for work and one for rest. Find out about how long your average task will take and then break that down into shorter increments. This will give you the sense that you are often taking a break but also making significant progress at the same time. Historically, most people go for using 25-minute work intervals and 5-minute rest intervals. After a few cycles of this, you can look back at your work and wonder how you got so much done yet feel so rested.

Email Best Practices

One of the most distracting activities while working is constantly checking your email. Studies prove that compulsively checking your email wastes more time than checking your email a few times and replying to your emails in one sitting. This goes the same for phone calls. Make sure to get all your phone calls done at once. Another way to save time while checking your email is to construct an effective and all-encompassing template. Having an effective template allows you to quickly reply to emails without wasting time to type out a new message every time with generally the same content.

In addition, make sure that you are using a proper email signature so you don't have to waste time rewriting your name and phone number on every reply. This also prevents the recipient from having to ask another question that you then have to waste time replying to. Ideally, you would want to check email no more than two times a day and email should not be the first thing you check in the morning. SaneBox is a nifty tool that can filter your emails based on their importance and help you save valuable time.

Goals

Setting and tracking goals is one of the most important things when you're running your own show. The smartest way to achieve this is by making sure that you have small benchmarks between your long-term goals to ensure that you are making efficient progress. For the busy entrepreneur, there are multiple apps that can help you do this.

Setting realistic goals is the key to success. For example, instead of setting a goal to reach a revenue of $1 million in two years, you can set a smaller goal, like reaching revenues of $100,000 in the next two months. This way, you will feel motivated and accomplished as you will be constantly hitting these mini goals in order to reach your bigger goal.

Another important thing to keep in mind is to set action oriented and measurable goals. To give you an example, instead of focusing on, say revenue, set a goal to make 10 sales call every day, which will automatically lead to increased revenues. That way, you are in control of doing that action and if you don't do it, you know you have failed.

Working Based on Your Body Cycle

You know how some people like to get up at 5am, go for a run and they are in the office by 7am? Or some people sleep in until 10am and don't leave the office until 9pm? Some people call this the difference between a morning and night person. More specifically, this is breaking down which body cycle they find themselves most efficient in. Dr. Michael Breus, popularly known as the Sleep Doctor, often speaks about how working during the correct body cycle can make you a more efficient person. He shows that people who work during their peak hours tend to get more work done than those who try to work against their own body cycle. For example, if you find yourself more of a morning person, it is best to capitalize on this feeling and schedule your appointments and more tedious activities for that time of the day. This allows you to operate at your highest efficiency during your most difficult tasks. Likewise, someone who tends to be more of a night owl should schedule their more difficult or tedious tasks during the later part of the day when their body has had time to adjust to the work. On Dr. Breus' website, you can find an in-depth quiz that will show you your most efficient body cycle. It's called The Power of When Quiz and it's totally free to take.

Stop Picking Up the Phone

Your day has been scientifically and meticulously planned out to the minute and the last thing you need to derail this train of efficiency is an unexpected phone call. This is where a personal assistant can also come in handy. Picking up a phone call distracts you from the task at hand and destroys your concentration. So, to avoid such a detriment to your day, don't pick up a phone call unless you've scheduled a phone call. Have the caller leave a message with your assistant and get back to them at your earliest convenience. Have your secretary trained on what an important or emergency call should be on the off chance that you receive one throughout the day.

Stay Healthy

When was the last time you heard of a sick person that ever got anything done besides finishing a bottle of Nyquil and a box of tissues? This may seem like a no-brainer but making sure that you are in good health is a must. As an entrepreneur grinding your way to the top, you cannot afford to take a day off or miss an important meeting because of a cold or a flu. Not only should you take your vitamins and wash your hands, but you need to make the time to exercise and get regular checkups. Don't just go to the doctor after you are sick because then it is too late. Your schedule had to be amended and you lost a client because of it. Your body is like a car. You run yourself ragged every day and once in a while, it is good to have a tune up.

Making Deadline and Cancelling Appointments

Making deadlines are what keeps us on track and what help us achieve our goals. If we only did things when we wanted to, tasks would never get done and businesses would never get off the ground. Setting personal deadlines for yourself and sticking to them will give you a sense of accomplishment as well as allow you to stay on track.

On the same note, you should also know how to prioritize your tasks. Knowing when a task is important is a valuable skill to have. Having lunch with a friend or finishing a project should not have equal precedence. A good way to know whether something is important or not is gauging your willingness to cancel that task or appointment. If you feel that something can be canceled, it more than likely should be canceled.

Impact vs. Effort

Through this section, we've been discussing the process of how to achieve efficiency but it is about time we put a name to this technique. The impact vs effort process gives a primer on how to prioritize and know how helpful the task you are performing will be in the long run. You have to ask yourself if your time is best spent performing this menial and tedious task that could be outsourced to a freelancer, or would it be best for you to have dinner with a potential business partner? The impact of creating a new business partnership far outweighs the effort of writing a new blog post for your website. This is a lethal time-saving technique that all entrepreneurs should implement into their process.

Identify Your Hurdles

Everyone has the tendency to procrastinate. We want to put off doing the things that are most unappealing to us. But as an entrepreneur, you have to tackle these uncomfortable tasks head on if you want to be successful. A good way to do this is by identifying what the hardest tasks of your day will be. By doing this, you can begin to prioritize and delegate your time to different projects in an intelligent manner. It is often recommended to do the most important tasks first so you don't spend more time on small tasks because of unconscious procrastination. This also relates back to the body cycle technique we talked about earlier. Some people do better when they quickly knock out the easiest tasks first giving them the fire and motivation to take on the hard tasks with a new fervor.

Using Cloud Based Services

Centralizing all your important online and shareable documents is one of the best ways to save time throughout your day. Dropbox and Google Docs have been cornering the market on efficiency and convenience in recent years. Storing documents on different computers can slow a business owner down in the long run. Google Docs provides an online solution to this problem by offering services similar to Microsoft Office but on an online platform. Google Docs provides spreadsheets, word documents, and slideshows that can be accessed from any computer around the world. So, instead of carrying that pesky laptop to every meeting, you can just upload your files to Google Docs and access them from any computer with an Internet connection.

Running Multiple Businesses and Building a Team

Do you own several businesses? If your answer is yes, you most probably know what it is like to be really overwhelmed. Running multiple businesses simultaneously and in the wrong way not only leads to low productivity, but also to failure in all the projects. This isn't necessarily the case, however - see Richard Branson and Amazon's Jeff Bezos.

Success starts with the right attitude

According to Napoleon Hill (Author of Think and Grow Rich), you can achieve whatever your mind conceives and believes to be possible. Therefore, you need to have the attitude that the job can be done and teach your team likewise. In this regard, you and your team need to view the workload as an opportunity to build a company as good as Branson's Virgin.

Come up with a plan

You have probably heard that a business lacking a plan is a business planning to fail. Therefore, you need to have a comprehensive business plan covering all the important aspects of your businesses. Among other things, your business plan needs to contain the following key aspects:

- A description of the products and services offered in each of your business ventures.
- An overview of the cost of all the inputs required in each of your businesses.
- A good sales and marketing strategy for all your businesses.
- A description of the staff and management in each of your businesses; this is basically a list of all the workers and supervisors and their roles.
- A strategy for advancement of each of your businesses, or future prospects.

Monitor all your businesses closely

It is important that you monitor each of your businesses carefully, to ensure that all the tasks are done on time. Whenever a vital task is assigned to an employee, request him/her to regularly update you on the progress, so you can estimate the efficiency with which work is being done. Also encourage team spirit among all your employees, so that tasks can be carried out more effectively. Let your employees know that it's okay to consult with you regarding any work matters.

One step at a time

This basically means that you need to focus on one task at a time. For instance, you may decide that this week will be dedicated to improving certain aspects of products in your business, while the next week will be meant for marketing and promoting. This is a tested strategy and it mostly works perfectly. Therefore, align your organization's activities in a uniform manner that can help you take a step at a time.

Build a team

The more businesses you run, the more you will need to build and manage a team. This is the best way to run multiple businesses, as your team will help you with management. After building this team, you need to treat them with passion and constantly motivate them to work towards achieving the end goals of your organization. Most of the incredibly successful entrepreneurs are very strict when it comes to hiring; they require nothing short of raw talent. Your team is what will make or break your business; make sure you have a good one.

Regularly perform internal financial reporting

Running multiple businesses is no mean feat and preparing financial reports is a task that you will need to complete frequently. Financial reports like balance sheets and income statements help you account for every buck in your business. This not only helps you avoid money wastage but also helps you know the profitable areas of your businesses, so you can capitalize on them.

Multiple Income Streams

One business is good for a start

If you are looking to go into business, you need to know that managing a business can be quite daunting and demanding. Therefore, you need to start with one income stream or business. This will not only help you gain experience in managing your ventures but also prevent you from overloading yourself with excess tasks. Following several months or years of operation, you will be well equipped with skills to deal with multiple-business management.

Consider future prospects

Jeff Bezos owns and operates several business ventures, including Amazon, The Blue Origin and The Washington Post. It was clear from the time he started Amazon that he always had future prospects. As an entrepreneur, he has stayed productive with all his ventures because he always considers the future, to fill any gaps in the market by providing that which is absent or being inadequately provided. Therefore, you need to have insight into the future, coming up with innovative products that will be received very well by the consumers.

Pick your business partners wisely

When your business grows, it becomes apparent that you are successful. A lot of people and even other organizations will want to partner up with you. However, you need to be very careful with who you choose to work with. Do a proper background check for everyone before entering into any partnership with them. Moreover, don't work with those who don't share your vision and mission; they will most probably lead you down the road of regret.

Learn to work with freelancers

In other words, this means that you need to outsource help for some of your critical tasks. As a matter of fact, freelancers are sometimes much more skilled than full-time employees. Here are some common tasks most suited to outsourcing:

- Web design and development
- Bookkeeping
- Content writing
- Admin tasks
- Graphic design
- Software development
- Customer support

Create a To-Do list

In any multitasking activity, a to-do list always comes in handy. When it comes to operating multiple businesses, having a to-do list is the best way to ensure smooth running of all operations. You could use a piece of paper or download a to-do app to help you prioritize your tasks. By having a to-do list, you'll be able to manage your time and be able to attend to all your business ventures effectively. Here are some pointers to help you create an effective to-do list:

- Review your emails every-day and prioritize based on urgency.
- Review the needs of each of your businesses to figure out which ones needs to be attended to first.
- Consider which tasks are most profitable; place them higher.
- Revisit your to-do list to discover which tasks have been accomplished; mark them as done.
- Try as much as you can to stick to your to-do list and ask your team to do the same.

- Prioritize the tasks that relate to your clients.
- Include time to look at your websites and social media accounts and reply to clients' queries.
- Don't let a task that pops up during the day ruin your whole to-do list.
- Reward yourself and your employees after accomplishing a difficult task; you could throw a party to celebrate.

Consult with other successful entrepreneurs

Do you personally know any entrepreneurs who run multiple businesses? You could try borrowing some tricks from them regarding operating multiple businesses and still getting it right with all of them. On the other hand, try to refrain from people who constantly try to discourage you saying that it is impossible to successfully run many businesses at the same time. Remember, many other entrepreneurs are doing the same and they have succeeded beyond measure and in ways that the average person cannot fathom.

Exploit your own skills

Are you a good professional auditor? Or do you have something you can do perfectly? Then consider doing it personally rather than hiring someone else to do it. The exception to this comes when the workload becomes too huge for you to handle.

Diversify in choosing your team

It would be great to have a whole team of pastry chefs in a hotel business. However, the business will certainly require other types of chefs, for instance short-order chefs and line chefs. When it comes to hiring your employees, consider having people with different skills suitable to your businesses. If, for instance, you are hiring accountants, you could consider hiring different types of accountants to suit all your accounting needs, for example: tax experts and cost accountants.

Keep your spirits high

When managing multiple businesses, things may not always go the way you want. Furthermore, it may seem that there are too many tasks or too difficult tasks. However, this is the same feeling most of the successful business owners like Warren Buffet have had to face when trying to operate multiple businesses. This is not to say that everyone who starts multiple businesses succeeds; of course there are those who don't. The difference between those who fail and those who succeed like Warren Buffet, is the willingness to keep going.

Bring your team together

Every once in a while, organize a get together for all your team members from all the businesses you are running. This way, all your employees will be able to pitch in to tackle certain pressing issues. Furthermore, they will be able to work as a family for the greater good of your business empire.

Allocate particular roles to each team member

You need to get it right when it comes to assigning tasks to teams or groups of employees when you're running multiple organizations. In this regard, you could consider doing the following:

Clearly outline the members assigned to a particular task. This step seems pretty simple and that's why most entrepreneurs often overlook it. This often leads to lack of cohesion among the team members, therefore resulting in tasks not being done properly. You need to ensure that all the members of each group know who they are working with. Furthermore, you need to encourage them to work together as members of a family with the end goal of achieving the set targets.

Research shows that the biggest cause of failure in most business teams is the lack of clarity of roles. In his book about increasing team productivity, Glenn Varney explains the usefulness of clearly understanding the specific tasks assigned to each member in a team. He stresses the idea that each member in a team needs to know his/her role, for which he/she will be held accountable. By knowing their roles clearly, team members are therefore empowered and encouraged to support each other.

Clearly outline the objectives of each task

When people are given tasks without any clear definition of objectives, the results are bound to be quite poor. On the other hand, goals act as a map to guide people on the direction to take and areas in which to dedicate their energy. Therefore, by setting targets, you will be challenging the team members to overcome all obstacles to ensure that they achieve the end goal of the task assigned to them.

Encourage employee feedback

By allowing employees to talk to you or your managers about the issues facing them, you inspire them to be more productive and honest in their work. This also helps to reduce gossiping among team mates, therefore increasing their productivity. The following are some ways of encouraging employee feedback:

Creating an email exclusively dedicated to getting suggestions from employees.

Positively acting on employees' suggestions.

Allowing employees to choose who they would like to give feedback to, for instance a certain manager.

Personally talking to them to let them know that they are free to speak their mind.

Streamline communication channels

To give you food for thought, communication errors made by medical personnel lead to more deaths than most major diseases. That's how serious communication errors can be; therefore, you need to clearly define the communication channels used by your teams and make sure they all exist. This not only reduces the probability of occurrence of errors, but also boosts efficiency. This would be even more helpful when you have team members in different countries across the world.

The greater picture

Employees are more productive when they learn that their efforts go beyond the purpose of making profits for the business; they therefore would like to see some of the profits realized through their hard work put to good use for the greater good of the society, for instance by helping the poor or starting foundations for research.

Know your employees

Working with employees in your various businesses is similar to cooking, with you as the cook and your employees as the ingredients. You would probably agree that you cannot cook prior to knowing your ingredients (even if we're talking about making pizza). The same case applies with operating your businesses. You need to relate personally with your employees to know their names, strengths and challenges, among other things. This way, you'll be able to work with them more effectively and they will be willing to go the extra mile for you.

Listen and learn from your employees

Most bosses are constantly telling their employees what to do; they seldom give their employees room to say something. As a matter of fact, employees find this situation annoying and demoralizing and can make them less productive. Therefore, it would be good to give your employees room to share their opinion. Rather than questioning them harshly regarding their actions, let them tell you what they feel; they may as well give you the next million-dollar idea.

Encourage innovation

It is true that you may have laid down procedures for how work is done in all your organizations. However, it is not following the rules that creates billion-dollar businesses; it is breaking them (of course in a reasonable manner). Therefore, encourage your employees to improvise ways of getting things done. How exactly can you do this? Ask them what tools they need in order to innovate something and provide them with the tools needed. Also, consider offering your employees incentives to encourage innovation and creativity.

Give a sense of ownership

Accountability is what sustains the performance of employees. However, performance doesn't last long when employees feel as though they are working hard just to enrich organizations that will never benefit them beyond the work contract. Therefore, the best way to maintain accountability and subsequent performance is giving your employees a sense of ownership. You need to allow them liberty to take charge of various tasks without you being there to supervise. This way, you will have created a sense of trust, and thus encouraged accountability.

Appreciate good performance

It is okay to praise employees and applaud them for a job well done, but there is more to that if you really want them to feel appreciated. Therefore, try to install systems for rewarding good performance of employees. For instance, you could offer them early paid leave, job promotions, gifts and so on. This will not only render them willing to perform even better next time, but it will also encourage other employees to work harder and achieve similar appreciation.

A chance for personal development

Leaders have used many means to make employees more productive, but the method that perfectly works to enhance performance is giving employees an opportunity for personal growth, especially in their profession. Therefore, you need to consider dedicating some time to helping your employees develop. You could do this, for instance, by hiring mentors to coach your employees. Another great strategy would be to provide access to study and training materials; you could even set up a library in each of your businesses.

Remember as we said at the beginning, success starts in your mind. Having a success-oriented mentality is what helps people like Bill Gates and Jeff Bezos succeed in most of their business ventures. We have one simple task for you – get Napoleon Hill's Think and Grow Rich; it will offer you enough motivation and fuel throughout your career as an entrepreneur.

Conclusion

Thank you for reading! We've found that this simple three stop process is a great roadmap to build new income streams. If you give it a go, we'd love to hear your feedback. We wish you the best of luck in your multiple income streams journey.

Thank You

We'd like to thank you again for purchasing this book.

There are a ton of books out there on building income streams and still you chose to spend your money on this one.

Hopefully, the knowledge that you gained from this book will help you start and run a smarter and more profitable business.

If you have any questions or feedback, feel free to drop an email at mohit@mohittater.com or dan@danmking.com

Your comments are very valuable as they will help us tailor content to your preference in our future books.

Thanks so much!

Printed in Great Britain
by Amazon